THE PRINCE
NICCOLO MACHIAVELLI

Machiavelli's *The Prince*
Available from bookstores

Please ask your local bookstore and library to carry this title
ISBN 978-0-996767705

eBook available from AdagioPress.com and WilliamDeanAGarner.com

The Prince isn't just for princes who thirst for, or are forcibly thrown into, advancement. It is a raw and bloody field manual for upper- and mid-level managers on predatorial ethics and power: what it is, how to obtain it, and what to do with it once you have found, stumbled across, or been granted it.

Edited by William Garner
New York Times bestselling ghostwriter/editor

Sun Tzu
Art of War
Ancient Wisdom . . . Modern Twist

"Dean Garner's version of *The Art of War* confirms
for us that for the past 2,000 years the fundamental
principles of special operations in battle have not
only remained true, but they apply equally to today's
boardrooms and bedrooms. When on the hunt or
holding ground, success can only be had by the pre-
cise application of disguise, deception and diversion,
and a genuine appreciation for angles, inches, and
seconds. Ranger Garner masterfully shows us how."

—Dalton Fury
New York Times bestselling author of
Tier One Wild and *Kill Bin Laden*

adagio

Sun Tzu *The Art of War*
Available from bookstores

Please ask your local bookstore and library to carry this title
ISBN 978-0-985536275

eBook available from AdagioPress.com and WilliamDeanAGarner.com

This contemporary edition of Sun Tzu's timeless masterpiece has
been edited down to its bare essence. It is just as, if not more,
relevant today as it was 2,500 years ago. The wisdom of *The Art of
War* teaches us that war is unnecessary. Peace is always the goal.

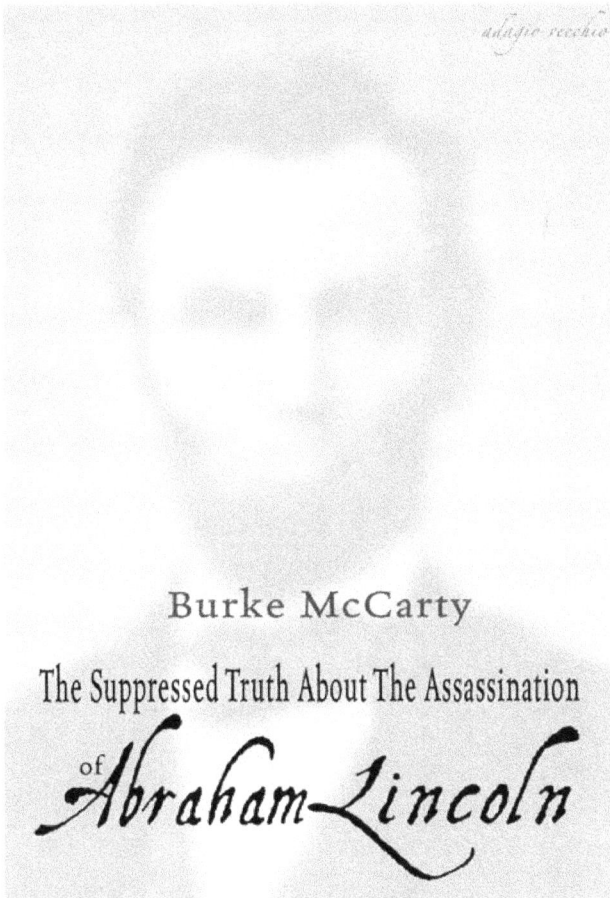

Burke McCarty

The Suppressed Truth About The Assassination

of *Abraham Lincoln*

The Suppressed Truth
About the Assassination of Abraham Lincoln
Available from bookstores

Please ask your local bookstore and library to carry this title
ISBN 978-0-996767712

eBook available from AdagioPress.com and WilliamDeanAGarner.com

Burke McCarty was a courageous ex-Catholic who conducted diligent research on the details surrounding the murder of President Abraham Lincoln by the Jesuits.

WILLIAM GARNER

WHO REALLY OWNS YOUR GOLD
How The Jesuits Use Gold Economics To Control Humanity

adagio

adagio

69-Minute Books   *a'vecchio*

AN INDEPENDENT PUBLISHING CRUISE
est. January 1, 2001

William Dean A. Garner
Editor

Published in the United States by Adagio Press

Adagio / 69-Minute Books colophons are Trademarks of
William Dean A. Garner and Adagio Press

Library of Congress Control Number: 2011917828

ISBN 978-0996767774

Printed in the United States of America

Book layout, design and covers: © William Dean A. Garner
Adagio website: http://adagiopress.com
Adagio email: 69@adagiopress.com

B20161116
Fourth Edition

for

Olga Marie Ramirez
1934-1992

Thank you for teaching me the accurate meaning of $e = mQ$...
An infinitesimal amount of mass yields unlimited energy

———◦✦◦———

Eustace Clarence Mullins
1923-2010

Thank you for discovering the real Oz, pulling back the oily black curtain, and
revealing those who are, at the moment, in control

———◦✦◦———

Sister Maria Monk
1816-1849
Never was there a more brave soul. Thank you for leaving behind your
experiences and thoughts and beliefs about what truly was,
and still is to this day, hell on earth. . . .

The thoughts, ideas and facts herein are dedicated to every Universal Patriot who *commands* a full accounting from elected leaders . . . *dares* to be free from the bonds of despotism and oppression . . . *exercises* the Universal right to a grand life . . . *demands* full liberty and the safety in which to practice it . . . and bravely *pursues* happiness to its fullest and most joyous.

—William Dean A. Garner
Cape Town, South Africa

Contents

Contents

Praise from We The People   xv

Acknowledgements   xix

Foreword   xxi

Introduction   xxv

Chapters

  0 *Another Tell-All Book About the Manipulation of Gold?*   1

  1 *The Golden Confidence Game*   7

  2 *The Great American Nightmare*   13

  3 *It's Deja Vu All Over Again*   19

  4 *Squeezed In A Vise, No Way Out*   25

  5 *The Curious Power Of Gold*   31

  6 *The First Great Gold Rush*   35

  7 *He Who Controls The Gold Makes All The Rules*   39

  8 *We The People Are Still Comatose*   43

  9 *Money Out Of Thin Air?*   47

10 *Is It Gold . . . Or Is It Tungsten?*   51

11 *Another Insider Blows The Whistle*   55

12 *What Can We The People Really Do?*   59

13 *And Now, Behold The Great Collapse*   65

14 *Why Should We The People Care?*   69

15 *Please Don't Shoot The Messenger*   77

16 *They Really Own Your Gold, America*   81

Postscript   91

About The Author   92

A Note On The Bibliography   92

Canada-US Civil Assistance Plan (CAP)   92

Bibliography   105

Praise from We The People

"Only an asshole tries to rewrite history. Fuck you and yours."

—Anonymous
New York, New York

———————————

"In this short, easy-to-read book, the author William Dean A. Garner asks: 'How many dots will it take you, Dear Reader, to realize that you are in the grip of an otherworldly, destructive force whose goal is to enslave you and your family?'

"It was in 1790 when Mayer Amschel Rothschild said: 'Let me issue and control the nation's money and I care not who writes the laws.' Now Garner connects the dots for you and explains how: 'We The People of the United States of America are in the worst predicament of the history of this country. And, perhaps worse, most of us don't even know it.'"

—Scott Oliver
Author of *How To Buy Costa Rica Real Estate Without Losing Your Camisa*
and *Costa Rica's Guide To Making Money Offshore in Bull & Bear Markets*,
and founder of WeLoveCostaRica.com

"I have read the book twice. It was extremely informative and easily understandable hard-hitting information. You have single-handedly solved the problem of important information being overlooked due to lack of time a reader has to spend reading a lengthy book.

"I would like to say thank you for taking the time and effort to write this book. You have created a vital weapon of knowledge that can be used against the TFSI.

"I believe that the format in which the book was written is the future of the way people will read, considering people's hectic lives.

"I read the book and wrote this email on a smartphone. The future of books, I believe, is in the ever-expanding world of digital technologies such as Kindle, smartphones, etc. So once again the hour or less read is going to become how people get information. I hope you are writing more books like this about other very important topics.

—Ian Smith
Sarasota, Florida

"Dino, thanks for letting me read the advance copy. You're not the first person to talk about how gold is manipulated, but you are the first person to put it all into one compendium and make sense of it all. Thank you very much. What's next?"
—Brad Jones
Albuquerque, New Mexico

"You have no clue what your talking about, Mr. Garner. Try another profession."
—Anonymous
Dallas, Texas

"The pope's Federal Reserve Bank owns all American gold. FDR deeded the gold to the Fed back in 1933. Curtis Dall has much to say about this in his book, FDR: My Manipulated Father-In-Law."
—Eric Jon Phelps
Pennsylvania

"Dean, I can't comment on this manuscript and you know why. I will, however, spread the word to everyone I know."
—Anonymous

———◦◦◦◦———

"Best information out there on this subject. Mr. Garner nails it completely. It should scare you to the core."

—Gold Is Money Forum

———◦◦◦◦———

"I've been day trading on the Street for 16 years and have heard rumblings and rumours about the things you write about here. Not sure what to believe anymore but I do know this...I'm going to be querying more than I did before thanks to this book and your sleuthing. I don't think you should have made it so short, though I get why you did--no one in America wants to read these days. In England, we read all the time. Must be the weather. Personally I rather would see a lengthy explanation of every chapter except one or two and who these [Jesuits] are. In one section you mention Romanic depression. The Pope? The Vatican? I don't think anyone would believe that. All I can say is...thanks."

—Anonymous
Greenwich, Connecticut

———◦◦◦◦———

"Dean, when I first ordered your book I was skeptical. But when I read it, everything made sense. So I looked up a few things you talked about in the book and found them to be true. I like how you use We The People as the 'good guys' in this David and Goliath story. Everyone should read your book, but I now know why most won't, especially those here in Mexico."

—Anonymous
Mexico City, Mexico

———◦◦◦◦———

"Mr. Garner, you were right all along. We are now halfway into 2014 and it's worse than you wrote about, but the mass media machine covers it up so we don't see it. Did you know there are 100 times more TV shows in 2014 than 10 years ago? More distractions to keep us occupied and not looking for clues that you wrote about. And still few people are listening."

—John Banks
via email

Acknowledgements

No author writes a book in a vacuum. Never happens. Even those authors who claim to write alone and by the golden glow of a single candle have their own rich and lively subconscious to guide them along, not unlike having the shadow-presence of Meyer Amschel Rothschild, Alexander Hamilton, Franklin D. Roosevelt and Ben Bernanke accompany them on their spirited journey.

When I write, I shake all the dust out of my head, summon the greatest minds in history to my room, serve an all-you-can-eat buffet of wine, beer and whatever kibbles I can throw together, and simply sit back and listen to them as they regale us with their experiential experiences and wisdom.

I am little more than a note-taker and typist in all this, so I cannot take any credit for the final product. However, I definitely can give it out to those mortals like myself who assisted me in compiling this book. I kindly thank:

Jean Bush for her valuable research and contributions about Ft. Knox's missing gold.

Sterling and *Peggy Seagrave* for graciously answering all my questions and offering excellent comments about the history of gold trading and theft in America and abroad.

Chris Kitze for many lengthy conversations about geopolitics, and excellent comments about the content in this book. Thank you also for posting the original article, on which *Who Really Owns Your Gold?* is based.

Bill Murphy for several lively and lengthy interviews about a very sensitive topic, and for commenting about the content of the original article and book.

There are hundreds of superb researchers and authors out there who have contributed first-rate books, articles, monographs, hypotheses and theories about who really owns the gold in, and controls, the world. I thank all of them for allowing me to stand on their shoulders, see a little farther over the horizon, and develop new hypotheses, theories and, in the end, present accurate results.

Foreword

The mental attitude of our whole people has been so affected with skepticism that our businessmen can no longer deal with them in candor and fairness. Yet the competition in all lines of business has become so intense that it forces them to resort to all kinds of deception in order to get a mere living and meet their monied obligations.

This demoralization reaches the professional class, forcing them to all kinds of questionable practices to meet the high cost of living. Many of them are living dishonorably, unable to gain their self-approval, without which life is a failure.

We see high finance in a John D. Rockefeller, head of a trust declared by the United States Supreme Court to be a criminal conspiracy. Yet, when forced to take the witness stand, he is under the protecting care of three of the reputedly great legal luminaries of this country, who had prostituted their intellects for money, to keep him from telling the truth to the people.

We see the guardians of high finance represented in Joseph H. Choate, a former ambassador to England, J. C. Spooner, a former Senator of the United States, who had ostensibly represented the people most of his life in the Senate, and Francis Lynde Stetson, the legal advisor of J.P. Morgan in trust building and bond deals against the United States Treasury. This mighty trio, for a valuable consideration, appears against the interests of the American people to see that a partner of J.P. Morgan & Co. does not tell the whole truth before a Committee of Congress appointed to investigate the "Money Trust," affecting the circulating medium, that measures the value of the property of every man, woman and child in this country.

Yet these men are regarded as an ornament to the legal profession.

When we pass to the highest tribunal, the citadel of last resort, where the people might hope for justice, and we see the Supreme Court of the United States, by a usurpation of power, undoing the will of the people as embodied in an act of Congress in the interest of trust combinations and against that of the people.

This has become a great moral as well as economic question, and the evil effects are shown in the conditions of our whole people.

We see today millions crowded into our big cities where it is a physical impossibility for them honestly to earn enough to get three meals a day and a place to sleep. A great many in moderate circumstances realize that on account of the high cost of living it is impossible for them by hard work to earn enough to marry and establish a home. Therefore, millions of them live in unholy relations resulting in moral degradation.

Vernon M. Cady, lecturer of the American Federation of Sex Hygiene, made the following statement in his lecture delivered in Washington:

Mr. Cady declared that there are 300,000 registered white slaves in this country and that the police of various cities estimate that there are one million more not registered. He declared that every moment's delay in not stamping out the white slave traffic is not only costly to society today but to the human race of the future.

Home is the foundation of our moral and religious life. Home is the atmosphere of character building, and all conditions should conduce to this all-important end.

To multiply happy home is, therefore, the greatest achievement of human government and is essential to the upbuilding of the character of a people without which all forms of government will inevitably result in failure.

By this test the records and the facts already demonstrate our failure. A dishonest and economically false money system has created artificial conditions, bringing about a high cost of living that makes it a physical impossibility for the honest young men and women of today to marry and establish homes, although living in a land of almost boundless resources.

The statesman, so-called, and legislator will look upon this picture and admit its truth and straightaway shift the responsibility by saying it's a moral question and should be solved and remedied by the Church.

The Clergy will be much affected and preach Sunday sermons on the subject, thereby relieving themselves of any further responsibility, or by saying it is a political question and we should not meddle in politics.

What chance does the religion of Christ have as a moral force upon the people surrounded by such conditions?

I ask those who have assumed sacred obligations of being the representatives of God and responsible for the preservation of the Christian Religion, as taught by Christ, and the salvation of human souls, "What answer have you to make for these conditions?"

This has become a vital moral as well as economic question that no man on this earth can neglect and perform his simple duty as a citizen.

How far greater is the responsibility upon those who have openly dedicated this lives to the Christian Religion and the good of mankind!

The cause and remedy are plainly outlined in this production and a call is made upon every honest man who loves his family, his neighbor, his country, and his God, to put the remedy in force. The people must save themselves. Their representatives in Congress have been "weighed in the balance and been found wanting."

The vital question to be determined is: Shall the Government be controlled by the people or by the power of money? It is therefore a matter of deepest and most widespread importance to the whole people of the United States and to their latest posterity.

Under the present system we have become a nation of debtors, and the borrower is but the servant of the lender.

Millions of men every day in the year appear in the presence of the money-lender, not as a freeman asking for the use of money for which he is prepared to give good security and pay the lawful rate of interest, but like a supplicant asking for favors and the very manner of condescension and superiority with which the money-lender grants the loan carries with it an implied obligation, the borrower must be good, attend strictly to business, and be in sympathy with the objects of the banks or he will lose its accommodation in future.

Every man in this country should be in position to demand the use of money, the medium of exchange for all properties, as a right, not as a favor, and he who has the land be able to borrow money at the same rate of interest as he who has bonds, in fact, if there is any discrimination it should be in favor of the real producers and not in favor of the non-producers or bond-holding class.

In contrast to this we see millions of the real workers and producers cowering in the presence of the money changers, a class which the people themselves have created through Congress surrendering to National Banking Corporations the power to issue a credit currency whereby they control they money-system of the United States.

I would impress upon every voter that real money can be created only by an act of sovereignty, and that each voter is an individual part of that sovereignty as a creator of money and obligates himself through this act of Congress to redeem this money in his services and property.

My earnest purpose is to make every man in the United States realize his importance as a sovereign voter, and his dignity as an American citizen, and that the man is not the servant of the dollar in this Republic; but its creator and that his property is more important than money, the medium of exchange.

It should be borne in mind that the value of the American dollar does not depend upon bankers or gold, but upon the National wealth of the United States created by the people.

As a result of the present money-system discriminating in the favor of money-lenders—non-producers—gamblers and parasites, the population has drifted away from agricultural pursuits—and the cities are overcrowded with non-producers.

One of the direct effects of the remedy herein given would be, immediate relief and encouragement to the agricultural interests, increase the demand and value of farm lands, multiply individual homes and real producers—increase the food supply and reduce the high cost of living. Business communities would be built up in the different agricultural sections, close to the sources of supply. These prosperous communities would soon be linked together by rapid-transit facilities, where many of the amusements of the city could be reproduced without the evils and temptations of city life; this making life in the country far more attractive, and rapidly increase its population, this relieving the congestion of non-producers in the cities.

Men would then prosper according to their merit and not according to their ability and cunning to overreach each other. These natural conditions would build up individual character and that honest American manhood which should be the glory of our civilization.

It would relieve all classes of businessmen from that anxiety and strain put upon them by the uncertainty of being able to get money when they most need it in their business, or to protect the valuable equities in the property they have acquired.

Every man should read this book and call the attention of others to it. "Eternal vigilance is the price of liberty."

Thomas Cushing Daniel
in *The High Cost of Living: Cause-Remedy*, 1912

Introduction

When choosing someone to contribute the Foreword to this book, I asked many people whom they wished to see write it. Everyone had a different suggestion. No one name they put forward struck me as appropriate.

In the end, I asked myself a simple question: "Of all the authors of all the books and articles and papers I've read over the past 30-plus years, whose words most resonate in my mind, heart, body and soul?"

Thomas Cushing Daniel.

This Introduction is not an account of this great man's good deeds to We The People, but rather an brief explanation about why I chose to incorporate some of his hundred-year-old thoughts in *Who Really Owns Your Gold.*

As you read the Foreword, did it seem contemporary to you, save the names of the deceased and old-style literary conventions? Was his subject matter something we're seeing in the news and with our own senses right now? How could he have known about these events that now seem so eerily present?

In short, Mr. Daniel was witnessing a cycle of events perpetrated on We The People of the United States by a group of men who reside in what has been the seat of all world power for more than two thousand years: Rome.

No, not the Vatican.

Not the white Pope.

From the dregs of hell, these power-hungry Jesuits have largely used the same tactics and strategies over and over again. So much so that when one reads about the events of the sack of the Weimar Republic in 1923, or the Panic of

1907, or the Great Depression, all those words and thoughts could very well be describing the events now unfolding well into 2015, only dressed a little differently.

My wish for you is that you deliberate the facts of the case I present to you in *Who Really Owns Your Gold: How the Jesuits Use Gold Economics to Control Humanity*. After you deliberate the facts, please be fair and honest in your assessment, then pass on your new-found knowledge to your family, friends, acquaintances, coworkers and anyone who will give you an ear. Arming yourself with this knowledge is the first step, sharing it with others is Step 2. Doing something about it may be the most important step of all.

Mr. Daniel was kind and diligent and caring enough to take the time to share with us all his observations of 100 years ago.

We owe it to brave men like him, not to mention to We The People, to listen carefully . . . consider diligently . . . and act appropriately and swiftly, because it's already too late to change the current system. The best we can do now is to build a new and more-efficient one in our lifetime. . . .

William Dean A. Garner
Cape Town, South Africa, 2014

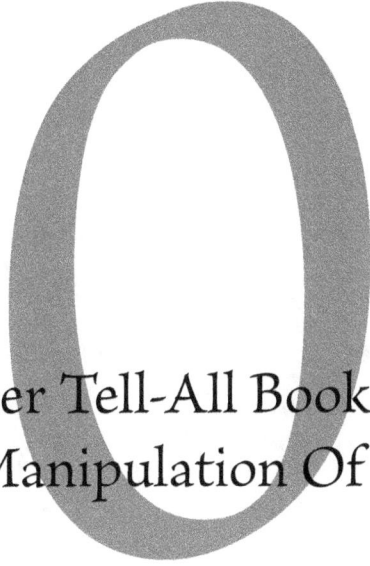

Another Tell-All Book About The Manipulation Of Gold?

If the American people ever allow private banks to control the issue of their money, first by inflation and then by deflation, the banks and corporations that will grow up around them will deprive the people of their property until their children will wake up homeless on the continent their fathers conquered.

— Thomas Jefferson

W hy write a book that will only stir controversy, not to mention precipitate pessimism and distrust in an atmosphere already infected by the current Great Depression, declining infrastructure, unnecessary wars, increasing propaganda, and rising apathy in our own children?

Simple: We The People of the United States of America are in the worst predicament in the history of this country. And, perhaps worse, most of us don't even know it because of all the mind- and body-numbing distractions all around us.

Worst and saddest of all, though: many know it in their gut but they dismiss it outright because it's at cross-purposes with what they've been taught in church, public schools, colleges, universities, and what they "learn" from BigMedia's so-called news, or what they believe to be true and accurate.

In short, our current dire situation conflicts with MTV, CNN, FoxNews, Entertainment Tonight, a thousand flavors of reality TV, the weekly bowling league, that haircut appointment on Tuesday. And with our own ignorance.

What follows is a message that should frighten you to the core. It's an object lesson that We The People should've learned 235 years ago when this fiasco first started in America, but evidently didn't understand enough to act on. Or, like our leaders, were too afraid to challenge because the powers that be, the Society of Jesuits, or Jesuits, threatened, bribed, assaulted or murdered them.

Even though We The People are showing up in the final hour, some members of our lot are truly catching on to the current economic state of affairs: the global economy and social condition suck. I say again: they suck.

Why?

Don't ask why. It's a philosophical argument I'm not prepared to defend, although Schopenhauer would say that we are so frustrated with our unfulfilled sexual desires that we destroy our surroundings.

Please ask *how*. It gets to the heart of the mechanics that underlie our current lot. That is something I'm well prepared to discuss and defend.

To my death. Yes, you read that correctly. My commitment to this undertaking is whatever it takes. That's the highest level possible. To the death . . . and not just my own.

How did we get all the way out to the thin ice where we're standing right now? Our crumbling infrastructure . . . shoddy elementary, high school, college and university educational systems . . . poor economy . . . poor collective health?

Among many other holes in the thin ice that has become our foundation?

How did we go from being the virgin continent with so much promise to the decaying and molding midden heap we live on today? True, there are patches of prosperity in America. There are some even in the darkest parts of Africa and Afghanistan. But the sum of our existence is less than zero.

It shows in our productivity, the strength of our dollar on the world market, and how other nations perceive us.

We got to this sorry state by thoughtful and careful design. Certainly not We The People's design, either. Rather, it's the work of a dark and sinister sphere of influence that the majority of us don't even know exists, let alone realize it controls us so tightly. When I mentioned the Jesuits on radio shows, I was ridiculed by some, those who turned out to be minions of the society. Thankfully, other brave souls saw through the Jesuits' veil of secrecy and deceit, and took it upon themselves to study this evil society.

I wrote this book over a period of 32 years. The first moment I realized something was amiss happened in 1980, when I was attending an embassy party in Washington, DC, where I was in college. After some period of moving from group to group, I was accosted by a well-dressed man of about 40, obviously frantic with some troubling thought on his mind. He said, and I'll never forget this: "He'll be the death of us all!"

"Who?" I asked, holding his hand earnestly.

He leaned into me and whispered loudly, "Brzezinski!"

Since that very moment, I have researched anecdotally for 32 years, and intensively for the last seven years, who really runs this world and how. Dr. Zbigniew Brzezinski is but one pawn on a grand chessboard of players whose aim is to dominate the entire planet.

The Jesuits' final episode officially commenced at the Congress of Vienna, Austria in 1814, and continued incognito with The Secret Treaty of Verona in November 1822, the articles of which were entered into record of the 64th Congress of the United States in 1916. Slowly, ever so slowly, their aim is to conquer our beloved republic, The United States of America. Worst of all, this once-slow pace has quickened considerably since the Internet and worldwide web have opened up new and unusual lines of fast communication among We The People and all good citizens of our planet.

We The People have one last golden opportunity to defeat the Jesuits, plus their accountants, the House of Rothschild and their extensive network of sycophants and minions. This current 69-Minute Book is but one dot in a constellation of stars that tells a grand story about our once-promising past, our dire present and especially our gravely uncertain future.

My hope is that you will take an hour or so and carefully consider this book's thoughts, ideas and beliefs. And when done reading and absorbing, you then digest its contents well, assimilate them into your very DNA, and then find a new strength to venture out into this beautiful world of ours and help it evolve positively and strongly.

If only by influencing one person at a time.

Please see through the veil of corruption that is the hallmark of the Jesuits and their semi-public face, the House of Rothschild. See through it and discover for yourself the true nature of these people's motives.

This volume introduces who really runs our planet and how they do it, using gold economics as a model.

As Jesuit lieutenant JP Morgan stated to the US Congress in 1912, "Gold is money. Everything else is credit."

While callously indifferent to We The People, Morgan was a man who knew the value of money, its power over people and industries and entire countries. So when he said that gold is money, he spoke it with a booming voice from high atop Mt. Olympus.

Not convinced? Consider this: these evil forces have backed We The People into such a corner that, even if we were taxed at 100% of our personal (not business) income, we still could never pay the interest on the "loans" forced on us by these evil forces. This puts us good people in a state of perpetual debt. No matter what we do, we are always in the red, always sinking below the surface, even though land is only feet away and, like a carrot at the end of a stick, always seemingly in reach.

When done reading this book and carefully considering the contents within, I kindly ask that you pass your knowledge on to those you love and care about. Educate them about the dangers they too will face in the near future if they do not act collectively and decisively against these forces of evil.

We The People are facing the most grim of events in our nation's history. While difficult to fathom now, especially since you may be experiencing isolated prosperity, what you are about to read is real. And frighteningly accurate and true.

Another book about the manipulation of gold.

Who needs it?

We The People, because this book is about more than just gold economics. It's about the manipulation of every sector of life across the globe by a dynastic group of men in Rome, who are successfully building a world that is counter to every good belief we hold dear and true.

1

The Golden Confidence Game

Creating money out of commodities like gold and silver and legislating value into them by making them legal tender us the worst possible policy and the greatest limitation placed upon advancing civilization.

—Congressman Charles A. Lindbergh
in *Banking and Currency and The Money Trust*, 1913

Gold and silver prices are being manipulated by a dynastic group of men who loathe you and want all your money and gold, even if it drives you to bankruptcy. Or suicide.

During the depression of the late 1920s/early '30s, the suicide rate jumped more than 50%. Don't be fooled, though: this wasn't The Great Depression that you've read about for decades. It was only one of a dozen previous "Great Depressions" this country has seen in the past 235 years, each one brought on by a unique combination of celestial-solar-lunar cycles and manipulated and exacerbated by a global power well hidden from We The People: the Jesuits and their accountants, the House of Rothschild.

And they're making their greatest power plays in 2012-2014, which will result in a global economic and social meltdown of epic proportions. And most of it will go unnoticed by all.

Regrettably, the subject of this current book does not cover the fascinating celestial-solar-lunar cycles, so I encourage you to buy and read one of the original books on the topic, *Cycles: The Science of Prediction*, by Edward R. Dewey and Edwin F. Dakin. Published in 1947, this ground-breaking volume was the first attempt in modern times (that is, after the 1880s) to examine how the influences of celestial bodies influence and directly modulate all life and geophysical events and processes on our planet.

Interestingly, only 65 years before Dewey and Dakin's book, in the 1880s, scientists and amateur astronomers/statisticians were actively reporting on these very cycles, but curiously all disappeared from the literature and were never heard from again.

Where did they go? Why were they suddenly removed from the consciousness of We The People? Did they hold some key to our lives and behaviors here on earth? Some clues that would be of great use to us? I do know one important item: those brave scientists who were at the center of study of celestial-solar-lunar cycles did not, all of a sudden, discover everything there was to learn about these cycles. Not by far. So . . . why aren't we studying them today?

The Jesuits have known about and manipulated these cycles for hundreds of years, almost always to the detriment of We The People, the good citizens of the United States of America. The Jesuits, through the House of Rothschild, surreptitiously removed all significant traces of previously reported studies and observations of the influence of these celestial cycles on earth. At least until Dewey and Dakin produced their seminal work.

Unfortunately, the authors did not reference previous work of those who had originally reported the influences of space events on life on planet earth. At that time, in the 1940s, the previous literature was devoid of such literature, having been secretly removed and destroyed by the Jesuits. The authors merely referred to other works and studies of repeating "business cycles" and "weather cycles."

The Jesuits have suppressed this and older work so We The People could not learn of it. They also continue to use this priceless knowledge to ride all major cycles and even influence and exacerbate them further to their advantage over the rest of us.

Two examples that matter deeply to you, Dear Reader: gold fixing and overselling.

The Jesuits been doing this for hundreds of years, printing fiat money out of thin air and selling precious metals, only to cry shortage and then offer you deflationary cash for your gold or silver purchase. They're the best at this con game and they've got it down to a delicate and accurate science.

In 2010, the Jesuits' minions, the House of Rothschild, were outed by Mr. Andrew Maguire, a metals trader in London who testified about JPMorgan Chase's shady trading practices.

Mr. Bill Murphy, Chairman of the Gold Antitrust Action Committee (GATA), published the following dispatch in support of Maguire:

"In November 2009 Maguire contacted the CFTC enforcement division to report this criminal activity. He described in detail the way JPMorgan Chase signals to the market its intention to take down the precious metals. Traders recognize these signals and make money shorting the metals alongside JPM. Maguire explained how there are routine market manipulations at the time of option expiry, non-farm payroll data releases, and COMEX contract rollover, as well as ad-hoc events.

"On February 3 Maguire gave two days' warning by e-mail to Eliud Ramirez, a senior investigator for the CFTC's Enforcement Division, that the precious metals would be attacked upon the release of the non-farm payroll data on February 5. On February 5, as market events played out exactly as predicted, further e-mails were sent to Ramirez while the manipulation was in progress.

"It would not be possible to predict such a market move unless the market was manipulated.

"In an e-mail on February 5 Maguire wrote: 'It is common knowledge here in London among the metals traders that it is JPM's [JPMorgan Chase] intent to flush out and cover as many shorts as possible prior to any discussion in March about position limits. I feel sorry for all those not in this loop. A serious amount of money was made and lost today and in my opinion as a result of the CFTC's allowing by your own definition an illegal concentrated and manipulative position to continue.'"

Now what? True, the *New York Post* chose to run the story about Maguire's revelations, but how far did that story get? What other insider confessions were on the way? To all intents and purposes, the story disappeared as quickly as it surfaced, and there were no follow-up stories in the *Post*. Why not?

"The Gold Cartel is running out of available central bank gold to meet the burgeoning demand," said Mr. Murphy in a separate interview.

Where does this leave the rest of us? When we want our physical gold from the bank or whatever entity houses it, what do we do when they offer us worthless dollars or euros? If we own gold stocks, this means we get nothing when we demand it.

Why?

Because the Jesuits order all its gold trading companies to issue much more stock than the actual gold it represents. It's called "fractional reserve." So when We The People make a run on the bank, we will get nothing because there will be nothing.

Here's the reality: the people who really own your gold and control our planet are the Jesuits, and they exert influence via their various minions and lackeys, in particular, the House of Rothschild.

2

The Great American Nightmare

"Credit has always been defined as loosely and as liberally as the multidimensional term fuck which, in its various incantations, has been used as a noun, verb, adjective, adverb, participle, gerund, bomb, torpedo, sword, knife, spear, pistol, screwdriver, drill, hammer, club, chariot, Trojan horse, shovel, backhoe, condom, dildo, tickler, or whatever grammatical, tactical, strategic, political or religious element possible under the sun and stars.

"Credit is anything remotely associated with funds, assets, capital, resources, cash, reserves, revenue, income, funding, backing, sponsorship, wealth, riches, fortune, affluence, lucre, resources, investment capital, goods, services, currency, hard cash, bank notes, bills, greenbacks, coins, change, dough, bread, loot, moolah, bucks, dinero, ducats, Benjamins, clams, ca-ching, and pesos.

"Money and credit are eerily analogous to mass and energy, as in $e = mc^2$. A small amount of mass can yield a huge amount of energy, like when a teeny bit of uranium^{235} went wildly meltdown and sacked Hiroshima and Nagasaki in 1945, and scared the holy shit (read: money) out of every nonconformist citizen across the globe.

"Likewise, a tiny amount of money can yield a huuuuge amount of credit, which yields even more money, yielding far more credit that becomes a self-perpetuating Godzilla, which consumes the world right underneath its own claws.

"With that liberal a definition and whimsical a practice of credit, it's no wonder America and the world are wildly broke as fuck and are currently in a runaway meltdown."

—William Dean A. Garner

The American Dream is dead and America is flat broke. We The People are so far in debt that we will never pay our way out, certainly not under the current laws and rules set forth by the Jesuits. That's not to say you still can't go out for a cold one after work each night, or rent a DVD and veg for hours in your overstuffed lounger in front of that cool 65-inch Samsung. Or get a world-class foot massage, manicure and pedicure on Saturday morning.

Even deep in the economic blood-red of the United States of America, there's always room for a six pack, a movie and a foot rub.

Way things are now, you can't possibly pay down all your bills in your lifetime, even though you probably worked out a plan to do so within 10 years, but that was 12 years ago when things weren't so bad and you had a full-time job with bennies and a small savings account, the IRA and the 401K and all that stuff you probably never thought you'd ever need.

Still high and climbing, your mortgage is overwhelming. The insurance on your home keeps creeping up year after year for no apparent reason, especially those of you who live in a state that demands flood insurance, or at least any sane reason the bank can give you, and you can't very well cancel it because the bank that holds your mortgage won't let you and they keep threatening you with immediate foreclosure if you as much as think about it.

With this new so-called healthcare reform now in place, your medical bills are skyrocketing, especially since your spouse went into the hospital with intestinal problems, and neither of you can afford health insurance because that would cost you both more than $2,000 a month in premiums, and neither of you takes home more than $1,500 after taxes every 30 days.

[Have you read the actual bill? Please do, because you'll see that the entity that suffers the most in penalties is the individual, another attempt to destroy the middle class.]

You have enough debt to saddle a medieval horse, and that horse's back is swaying more and more with each passing nanosecond. Any day now, it'll surrender to gravity like a droopy chin, and the once majestic beast will drown in a sea of debt that screams over you like a tsunami that traveled 10,000 miles from the dark, cold Antarctic, gathering more and more momentum with each passing mile.

Is there any recovery from such a force of nature?

The good news is that once you come out from under that bankruptcy, all those material things you accumulated over your lifetime—the beautiful home and the car and truck, and your worldly possessions—will be in someone else's hands, starting with your bank, which has no use for your stuff anyway except for what it might fetch at Auction Wars.

No more dusting off the little Hummel pieces from grandma. No more cleaning the fine silver you got on your wedding day from all your friends who chipped in money they didn't have. No more vacuuming and cleaning your lovely home you built from scratch and promised to pay down before the end of that 30-year, 6% loan.

You'll be left with little more than a few articles of clothing, if even those. Life is no longer what you thought it would be. The American Dream has fast become The Great American Nightmare, brought on by an invisible force some call dark matter or quantoretta, the stuff of science fiction that tells us we can't see it or smell it or touch it, but its effects are there and they're real so you best believe it.

And in the wake of all this, you're left scratching your head, wondering what the hell just happened here?

Does anyone have an accurate answer? Does anyone outside your life even care? Your friends have all but abandoned you, because they're in the same position, facing bankruptcy or having just been spat out by the court system that took everything they once owned. Daily phone calls that once beamed happiness and baseball and Oprah now scream and cry tales of IRS liens, foreclosures and that fourth job, the one that starts at two in the morning when the baby's crying.

Your family can't help you, either, because they just got hit with a huge tax bill that they'll never be able to pay, but hey, wait, there's always that monthly payment system with the IRS, and they only charge 30% interest on top of what they say you already owe them.

So, no, even family can't help you. Seems everyone you know is being pulled under by this black hole whose invisible and unyielding gravity takes no prisoners, but it's all too happy to take you down down down into that forever abyss.

The Great American Nightmare used to be the stuff of Edgar Allan Poe and Stephen King. Now it's front-page headlines even in mainstream media. No one can escape it.

The United States is going down that same road of hyperinflation and depression that effectively sacked the Weimar Republic in Germany, in 1923, and ushered in a new beast not seen in modern times: the secret Jesuit priest, Adolph Hitler, and the German National Socialist Party, the Nazis.

At that time, Germany was the most industrialized nation on the planet, a gleaming trait that soon turned to rust.

The grand purpose then was to corral all the citizens of the Weimar Republic, beat them into submission, and force a new way of life on them: fascism . . . cleverly disguised in the colorful party costume of friendly and benevolent socialism.

If We The People dare look at the facts, we will see the very same behaviors by the Jesuits playing out each day in each of our lives. The US used to be the most industrialized nation on the planet.

China now holds that distinction, and for good reason: since the 1950s, the Jesuits have systematically transferred manufacturing from the US to China, effectively crushing the ability of the US to build its own infrastructure. Now we must rely on an adversary for basic parts and supplies even for our high-tech military aircraft and ships.

Recently, it was revealed that a 30-foot-tall granite statue of Dr. Martin Luther King, Jr., now on prominent display next to the Washington Monument, was Made in China.

In the near future, when you call Wells Fargo or Walmart or some prominent business, you'll hear the following recording:

"For English, please press one . . . for Español, please press two . . . and for Chinese, please press three, four, five, six, seven, eight, or nine."

A sign of the times to come, and it's all be design. . . .

One only need connect so many dots of circumstantial evidence to see the pattern of abuse against us. How many dots will it take you, Dear Reader, to realize that you are in the grip of an otherworldly, destructive force whose goal is to enslave you and your family?

If you do not trust "circumstantial evidence," please consider this: there are only two ways to prove a conspiracy. One, the conspirators or whistleblowers come forward to admit or expose the deed; or some brave soul does sufficient research over many years and connects enough dots of this circumstantial evidence to arrive at an accurate conclusion that he then presents the world.

Unfortunately, it's impossible for you to stop the Jesuits and their handlers. It's been going on for hundreds, if not thousands, of years . . . it's happening as we speak . . . and it will continue well into your future.

The best you can do now is learn about it and try to avoid the pain and suffering, and perhaps pray for some external intervention. Another option is to build a whole new system, one that usurps the Jesuits' current one, but this would take a hundred years.

Although most would dismiss the idea, the only external entity capable of helping humanity now are extraterrestrials. . . .

3

It's Deja Vu All Over Again

"When the tyrants of the earth began to transgress the sacred line of property, and claim their fellow men as slaves, and to exercise lawless power over them, the intentions of government were subverted, war in defence of the dignity of human nature was introduced, and men began to take the field of battle on behalf of freedom."

—James Sullivan and Joseph Hawley
Principal Authors
in Broadside of the
Massachusetts House of Representatives
November 1, 1776

On the final day of the Weimar Republic's hyperinflation, 16 November 1923, one US dollar netted 4.2 trillion marks. This is not a typo. Four point two trillion marks sounds like a lot of money, and at one time it truly was. Unfortunately, it was little more than nicely printed toilet paper in late 1923, in the Weimar Republic.

During better times, the exchange had been four marks to the dollar. Inflation had skyrocketed to a dizzying 300 million percent. People were carrying sacks of devalued cash in their bags, baby strollers, grocery sacks, and stuffed into their clothes, to be used mostly as kindling and wallpaper.

"In October 1923 it was noted in the British Embassy in Berlin that the number of marks to the pound equalled the number of yards to the sun. Dr Schacht, Germany's National Currency Commissioner, explained that at the end of the Great War one could in theory have bought 500,000,000,000 eggs for the same price as that for which, five years later, only a single egg was procurable.

"When stability returned, the sum of paper marks needed to buy a gold mark was precisely equal to the quantity of square millimetres in a square kilometre. It is far from certain that such calculations helped anyone to understand what was going on; so let the un-mathematical reader take heart."

"The greatest loss which Germany suffered was the ruin of her middle classes."

This bears repeating: the overall result of the collapse of the Weimar Republic was the destruction of the middle class, which created two classes, rich and poor, very easy to control and manipulate.

The very same patterns from that depressing era are now upon us again, only dressed in different, perhaps more stylish, clothes this round. An engineering feat, the destruction of a once-strong and proud Germany in the early 20th century has visited the world dozens of times since the late 1770s. Curiously, this was shortly after Meyer Amschel Bauer founded his little banking institution in Frankfurt, Germany, and after the Jesuits were unceremoniously banished from certain ecclesiastical halls by Pope Clement XI and then later resurrected, only to begin a new reign of terror across the world but especially in the United States.

Bauer's father, Amschel Moses Bauer, hung a red shield outside his five-story house, signifying he was the go-to man for money changing and lending in town, a skill he passed on to Meyer Amschel. In short order, Bauer the younger's business flourished, and he wished to be more closely associated with it, so he changed his name to Rothschild. In German, rot means red; schild is shield. The Red Shield.

And so began the steady rise and secret reign of the House of Rothschild, under the strict iron hand of the Jesuits who, like their predecessors, have always used Hebrews and Khazarjews as their primary accountants, bankers and semi-public face, which seemingly gives We The People a target to focus on when frustrated, a target that is cleverly shifted from the real culprits, the Jesuits.

Over a 40-year period, Meyer Amschel Rothschild forged the most powerful banking system in the world, taking over the Bank of England, plus the major banks in France, Germany, Italy and Austria, and soon expanded outward like a slowly diffusing cloud of poison gas. Rothschild's five sons further scattered their father's demon seeds and established very potent banking cartels of their own.

In very little time, the Rothschilds established their own agents within many different European governments, and, under orders of the Jesuits, then set sights across the Atlantic on the United States, still wet behind the ears and eager for the affections of all suitors outside her virginal shores.

Perhaps the best depiction of international bankers and their plots against us was made by historian Dr. Carroll Quigley, who was given unique access to the secret activities of the Jesuits and the House of Rothschild in America and who, in the end, decided to rat them out in his book, *Tragedy and Hope*:

"Hundreds of years ago, bankers began to specialize, with the richer and more influential ones associated increasingly with foreign trade and foreign-exchange transactions. Since these were richer and more cosmopolitan and increasingly concerned with questions of political significance, such as stability and debasement of currency, war and peace, dynastic marriages, and worldwide trading monopolies, they became the financiers and financial advisors of governments.

"Moreover, since their relationships with governments were always in monetary terms and not real terms, and they were always obsessed with the stability of monetary exchanges between one country's money and another, they used their power and influence to do two things: (1) to get all money and debts expressed in terms of a strictly limited commodity—ultimately gold; and (2) to get all monetary matters out of the control of governments and political authority, on the grounds that they would be handled better by private banking interests in terms of such a stable value as gold."

The goals of these international bankers and the higher power they serve have since been accomplished. We need only step back in time, to 1913, when the US Federal Reserve Act was passed, effectively handing over control of the US's money supply, and its maintenance and distribution to the Jesuits.

To this very day, that same poison, manufactured and delivered by the House of Rothschild and those they serve infect America to the point of cancer and near-death. The Rothschilds are acting as financial and political agents for the Jesuits, but that's not the focus of this particular story.

We have seen our freedom and liberty stripped away like so much good, sturdy paint under a demon sandblaster. The government and its minions have been distancing themselves from the population, feeding more and more disinformation and propaganda to the masses, and silencing anyone speaking out against their ill deeds. After all, the Jesuits control all mass media and have since the late 1800s, when they directed the House of Rothschild to buy all influential media outlets across the globe. In the process, they also crushed smaller media companies and suppressed or destroyed any and all publications about the Jesuits. One is hard-pressed to find any books about the Jesuits, especially those published before the 1880s.

Let us bring our focus back to the subject of this book: global control via gold economics:

Two of the most courageous people ever to attempt to write on this subject are the husband-wife team of Sterling and Peggy Seagrave. In their well-researched book, *Gold Warriors: America's Secret Recovery of Yamashita's Gold*, they said the following about those in power:

"We live in dangerous times, like Germany in the 1930s, when anyone who makes inconvenient disclosures about hidden assets can be branded a 'terrorist' or a 'traitor.' [Some time] ago [~2002 or 2003], three ex-ambassadors to Japan declared that former American POWs and civilian slave laborers, suing Japanese corporations for compensation, were tantamount to terrorists. Now a CIA official says that leaks of classified information must be stopped, even it is necessary to 'send SWAT teams into journalists' homes.'

"Everybody's national security is a serious matter. We have no argument with that. But national security can be invoked to hide official corruption, and conflict of interest. It's called tyranny. The only cure is openness and sunlight."

Again, the US is going down that very same road to hyperinflation, destruction of the middle class, and loss of freedom and liberty. Our economy is slowly falling apart from the inside, as the middle class fades from view, only to be replaced by the poor at the bottom and the rich at the surface.

This scenario was played out similarly nearly 100 years ago in the Weimar Republic. The playbook is still the same, although the coaches and players have changed. And all those in the stands.

It is those dynastic men in Rome, the Jesuits, and their accountants, the House of Rothschild, hidden deep within their secret chambers, who are drawing the blueprints for all life at the surface where We The People anxiously reside and await our fate. . . .

4

Squeezed In A Vise, No Way Out

The little step, long continued–the very gradual but persistent advance–is sure to attain its end.

–Lord Robert Montagu

The 14th year of our new millennium has brought in new legislation on many levels. With the passage of the healthcare bill, which also mandates a new and higher taxation on those hard-working American citizens earning more than $200,000 a year, we're now seeing ever-increasing and sweeping "reforms" of our Constitutional laws and forms of civil protection.

Please consider the following klaxon issued by the American Civil Liberties Union:

> "On December 31, 2011, President Obama signed the National Defense Authorization Act (NDAA), codifying indefinite military detention without charge or trial into law for the first time in American history. The NDAA's dangerous detention provisions would authorize the president—and all future presidents—to order the military to pick up and indefinitely imprison people captured anywhere in the world, far from any battlefield."

The NDAA wholly and effectively destroys the rights of all citizens in all countries throughout the entire world. And the law isn't a universal one that was agreed upon by the citizens or governments of all countries; it was passed by the Congress, and signed into law, by the president of a *single* country: The United States of America.

More alarming at home, perhaps, is the appearance of the Transportation Security Administration (TSA) on our nation's highways, now expanding their checkpoints from airports. The TSA, modeled after the Nazi Gestapo, is "inspecting" weigh stations along certain highways, starting in the good state of Tennessee.

"Where is a terrorist more apt to be found? Not these days on an airplane more likely on the interstate," said Tennessee Department of Safety & Homeland Security Commissioner Bill Gibbons.

The passage and enforcement of the NDAA and the widening of TSA's checkpoint inspections are nothing new: similar measures were forced upon the citizens of Nazi Germany in a slow but methodical mission creep that ended in subjugation of the good people of Germany.

It will end with the capture and destruction of We The People's Constitutional rights, just as Lord Montague suggested nearly 150 years ago (out of context): "The little step, long continued—the very gradual but persistent advance—is sure to attain its end."

The Administration spins these laws and missions: they are called *reforms*.

Interestingly, too, all these "reforms" have risen before, in one state or another, in all countries hijacked by the Jesuits. What is very disturbing is that this enormous increase in personal income taxes is being falsely justified. The

Obama Administration claims that those very taxes from Americans, especially those earning more than $200,000 a year, will help fund America's healthcare reform.

The Administration's claim is not simply misleading, it is an outright lie.

America's personal income taxes are paid to the privately owned Internal Revenue Service, a registered corporation of Puerto Rico. One hundred percent of our personal income taxes are used to pay the interest on loans forced on the US by the Jesuits through the privately owned US Federal Reserve, which promptly sends those funds to the Bank for International Settlements (BIS) in Basel, Switzerland. All owned and controlled by the Jesuits. In 2010, I wrote an article that exposed the BIS by listing all countries that had a central bank (all central banks are owned by the Jesuits). Within a few short months, the BIS removed all traces of information, including the amount of money it collects each year from the US. Curiously, that amount is equal to the sum of all personal income taxes paid by US citizens.

The real design behind increasing taxes of the highest-earning Americans is to drain the strongest and most successful Patriot-Americans of their wealth at a more accelerated pace than in the past. Mind you, these Americans are not part of the Jesuits' global agenda. There are genuinely good, hard-working people who typically earn between $250,000 and about $1M a year and serve as the backbone of small business in the US.

Why drain the moderately wealthy now, though?

The Internet and all its derivatives allow more and more concerned citizens to learn about the dark machinations of the Jesuits, and pose a direct potential threat to their actions, especially with the emergence and increasing mainstream exposure of so-called "conspiracy theorists" that the current Administration seeks to identify, infiltrate and destroy.

Over the past 10 years alone, witness the passage of the Patriot Act, establishment of the Department of Homeland Security, passage of the healthcare reform bill, etc. All these measures have effectively dissolved the US Bill of Rights and our beloved Constitution.

I stated this earlier, but it bears another look: if you simply examine an electronic version of the new healthcare bill and do a search for "penalty" or "penalties," you'll soon discover that the entity that pays the most in penalties is the individual: We The People. This is one of the methods used to destroy the middle class of this country, the same tactic used in previous wars on populations around the world.

Look all around you, Dear Reader. Think about what you're observing in this country. Look deeper than you ever have before, and do good, solid research on your own. If you observe closely enough, you'll see some interesting, if not disturbing, methods.

The Jesuits tirelessly repeat their tried-and-true patterns of:

Demoralizing a public with depressing news in the mainstream media, plunging the nation into serious debt using controlled and manipulated recessions and depressions, low-income jobs and high unemployment, evermore controlling new laws and regulations that are increasingly intrusive to all citizens.

Destabilizing a population by pitting groups against each other, i.e. Democrats vs. Republicans or pro-choice vs. anti-abortion or gun owners vs. anti-gun citizens, in pitched battle. And when they can't corral those elusive holdouts who subscribe to no party or religion or group, the Jesuits create even further "controlled opposition," i.e. those people and groups who purport to be friends of We The People and who allegedly oppose the Jesuits, echoing their pro-We The People sentiments in high public places. The grim reality is that those final holdouts among We The People are cleverly being pulled into a black hole of false security by all the controlled opposition and false opposition.

Orchestrating crisis after crisis, e.g. internecine wars, regional wars, global wars, the Great Depression, the "War on Terror," 9/11 attacks, illegal attacks on nations like Afghanistan and Iraq, culminating in forced military occupation of those nations.

Forcing legislation that removes basic Constitutional rights. An excellent and unfortunate example: United Nations Framework Convention on Climate Change effectively destroys the entire US Constitution. Read it for yourself. The sweeping language is in English and it's easy to read and is quite digestible, although it will doubtless produce a severe case of diarrhea you won't soon forget. And don't forget the Patriot Act and NDAA.

Normalizing a population, allowing those in power to bring the American public under its sphere of influence, bringing to a screeching halt all protests a gainst the regime, eliminating all challengers, and thus fully squeezing We The People within an otherworldly vise.

We've seen this general template used in other countries, but how it will play out in 2014 and beyond? Will be have martial law? Will foreign troops occupy our soil? Will our own military be ordered to march against its own citizens and even fire upon We The People?

It's happening so slowly you don't notice it, America.

Like the unknowing frog, we are being boiled *alive*, one achingly slow degree at a time.

5

The Curious Power Of Gold

Gold is money.

Everything else is credit.

—JP Morgan
Testifying to US Congress, 1912

H istorically when Americans have felt an economic constriction, where the dollar has begun to lose so much value that even the People's Republic of China threatens to dump it like old bath water, they turn to the only precious resource on earth that has held at least some value, even in direst times: gold.

No one knows when gold was first discovered, but it started showing up about 5,000 years BC in various parts of the world: Central Europe during the Copper age, and in Egypt and Saudi Arabia during the Bronze Age, about 2,500 BC.

While gold may have had other uses when first discovered, it clearly was molded and shaped into many different artifacts, some of which have been discovered over the millennia. Ancient Egyptians worshipped gold, calling it a gift from the sun. Its sheer beauty and glamour, not to mention malleability, have enabled artists to fashion thousands of different styles of jewelry and other precious artifacts.

To say that humans have been mesmerized by gold for nearly 7,000 years would clearly be an understatement. Since its discovery, it has been the King of Trade the world over.

The human mind reacts to gold in a most reverent fashion, quite unlike it does to any other substance.

A Latin proverb faithfully expresses our potential for venality: "Even the just may sin with an open chest of gold before them."

Perhaps this proverb explains the inimical behavior of the Jesuits toward their fellow citizens of Planet Earth. Are the Jesuits so doped up on global control that they will do anything to lay claim to all the gold? In short, yes. And they and their predecessors have for thousands of years.

As far back as 4,000 BC, gold became prominent in what it is now Eastern Europe. It was used primarily for decorative ornaments and jewelry. It would not be until approximately 2,500 years later that gold would become a form of money. Egypt may have been the first country or region to officially establish gold as money to be traded for goods and services. They mined their gold from nearby Nubia (now Sudan).

Gold soon spread into the Middle East where the Shekel became the first recognized standard unit of gold measure: 75% gold and 25% silver, an alloy known then as electrum.

Over the millennia, gold has come and gone as a unit of money, a worldwide standard by which countries' currencies have been measured and normalized, and forged itself as an ever-present fixture in the high-tech and jewelry-manufacturing industries.

Unfortunately, goods and services normally cannot be paid for in gold, because large payments are impossible, unless one wishes to carry around tons of gold. The banking system came into play here, substituting bank notes and deposits for real gold. And that's where the "gold standard" also was instituted, although it too became a plaything for the Jesuits, which manipulated it as blithely as it did all currencies.

Lately, too, gold has become the weapon of choice the Jesuits wield to devalue a country's currency and cause severe, if not total, economic collapse. You now know who really owns your gold, so the next question is how do they use it to their advantage? Simple: manipulating and controlling global markets.

We are now in the 11th hour of an epic battle.

The discovery of gold in the US may provide some insight into the unique behavior of people under the influence of a precious, scarce and hard-fought resource with the power to create and destroy all that is good.

6

The First Great Gold Rush

Louis Remmé was a young French Canadian who came to the American West to seek his fortune in the cattle business. In February 1855, after a long drive, Remmé deposited $12,500 in gold with Adams & Co., then the state's largest bank and express company. He received a negotiable paper receipt, guaranteed to be redeemable in gold upon demand.

However, the cattleman was unaware of the widespread stock speculation then going on among banks and other companies. Adams & Co. was linked to a company that had invested heavily in a failed railroad deal. Unknown to Remmé as he deposited his coin in California, the bank had already collapsed on the East Coast.

Several weeks later, the steamer Oregon brought the news to San Francisco. Confusion reigned. Redemption of deposits ceased, and the branches of Adams & Co. Bank in California closed their doors forever. Hundreds of people were left with worthless paper certificates.

Suddenly, inspiration struck Remmé. Adams and Co. had a branch some 600 miles away, in Portland, Oregon that had not yet received the news. He lost no time in saddling his horse and heading north.

Meanwhile, the Pacific Mail Steamship Columbia left San Francisco, bound for Portland with the news. Riding through uncharted wilderness and hostile country, Remmé traded horses at every opportunity. He braved the rugged winter of the Cascades and was pursued and shot at by hostile Indians, but kept right on going. Remmé was determined to convert that piece of paper back into hard money.

Could the young cattleman outrun the Columbia before she docked in Portland?

Luckily, the steamship stopped to resupply a military fort along the way. Seven days after he left Sacramento, an exhausted Remmé rode into Portland and headed straight for the bank. He cashed the certificate for gold, more than happy to pay the agent's commission. He had beaten the steamer by just a few hours.

The other customers of Adams & Co. in Oregon remained in the dark until it was too late.

—Ralph Terry Foster
in *Fiat Paper Money: The History and Evolution of Our Currency*

The first gold rush in the US commenced on a rainy afternoon, on 24 January 1848, when James W. Marshall discovered gold on land owned by trader Captain John Sutter, who kept a diary of the events over the next decade. What he saw was an exercise in human greed.

Something else altogether emerged from the fracas: a display of American freedom and liberty. Each person who braved dangerous geography, weather and wild wild natives had come to the West because they knew that whatever they discovered, whatever they pulled from Mother Earth with their own hands and endless labor was theirs. And theirs to keep. The King would not be standing over them to collect his usurious 96% of their hard-earned pay. The Bank of England would not send out its collectors to threaten them with their signature penalty for nonpayment: drawing and quartering.

What Captain Sutter witnessed ruined him for life, and he never recovered. Buried deep among his pain and suffering, the good Sutter knew he was also eyewitness to the very pillars that helped build our great country: independence, and the absolute freedom to with it whatever he so chose.

That exercising of freedom is called *liberty*. Captain Sutter's entry for 28 January 1848 is telling, describing in detail a secret meeting with Mr. Marshall:

"Marshall arrived in the evening, it was raining very heavy, but he told me he came on important business. After we were alone in a private room he showed me the first specimens of gold, that is he was not certain if it was gold or not, but he thought it might be; immediately I made the proof and found that it was gold.

"I told him even that most of all is 23 carat gold. He wished that I should come up with him immediately, but I told him that I have to give first my orders to the people in all my factories and shops."

Mr. Marshall told his story in Hutchings' *California Magazine*, in November of 1857: "I am not quite certain to a day, but it was between the 18th and 20th of that month, 1848, I went down as usual, and after shutting off the water from the race I stepped into it, near the lower end, and there, upon the rock, about six inches beneath the surface of the water, I was entirely alone at the time. "I picked up one or two pieces and examined them attentively; and having some general knowledge of minerals, I could not call to mind more than two which in any way resembled this: sulphuret of iron, very bright and brittle; and gold, bright, yet malleable; I then tried it between rocks, and found that it could be beaten into a different shape but not broken.

"I then collected four or five pieces and went up to Mr. Scott (who was working at the carpenter's bench making the mill wheel) with the pieces in my hand, and said, 'I have found it.'

'What is it?' inquired Scott.

'Gold,' I answered.

'Oh, no,' returned Scott, 'that can't be.'

I replied positively, 'I know it to be nothing else.' "

Over the next year, Captain Sutter's land was overrun by squatters and other miners who collectively mined more than $40 million in gold. That figure rose to $55 million only one year later.

The first gold rush was on.

Soon after, General Sutter lamented over his predicament, in *California Magazine*, November 1857:

"Soon as the secret was out my laborers began to leave me, in small parties first, but then all left, from the clerk to the cook, and I was in great distress; only a few mechanics remained to finish some very necessary work. . . .

"Then the people commenced rushing up from San Francisco and other parts of California, in May, 1848: in the former village only five men were left to take care of the women and children. . . .

"What a great misfortune was this sudden gold discovery for me! It has just broken up and ruined my hard, restless, and industrious labors, connected with many dangers of life, as I had many narrow escapes before I became properly established. From my mill buildings I reaped no benefit whatever, the mill stones even have been stolen and sold. . . .

"By this sudden discovery of the gold, all my great plans were destroyed."

When gold diggers flooded California, they plundered and, like marauding army ants, were equal-opportunity rapists, thieves, muggers and killers: young or old, rich or poor, Americans or Indians. Chief Young Joseph of the Nez Perces shared his thoughts:

"For a short time we lived quietly. But this could not last. White men had found gold in the mountains around the land of winding water. They stole a great many horses from us, and we could not get them back because we were Indians.

"The white men told lies for each other. They drove off a great many of our cattle. Some white men branded our young cattle so they could claim them. We had no friend who would plead our cause before the law councils. It seemed to me that some of the white men in Wallowa were doing these things on purpose to get up a war."

Greed became commonplace, plunging America into a new era of industrialization that, by all rights, should've lasted a millennium but in grim reality would last less than 100 years because the hidden hand of the Jesuits directed our growth in a direction inimical to We The People.

7

He Who Controls The Gold
Makes All The Rules!

GOLD IS A CURRENCY.
GOLD IS COMPETITIVE TO PAPER CURRENCY.
GOLD IS NOT A COMMODITY.
GOLD IS A BAROMETER OF FEAR.
GOLD IS A BAROMETER OF CONFIDENCE IN GOVERNMENT.
GOLD IS INSURANCE.
GOLD IS INSURANCE AGAINST GOVERNMENT GONE MAD.
INSURANCE IS NOT SOMETHING YOU TRADE.
GOLD IS THE FINANCIAL HIGH GROUND WHEN GLOBAL
DEBT PROBLEMS EXIST.
GOLD IN YOUR HAND ELIMINATES ALL COUNTER-PARTY RISK.
EVERY SINGLE CURRENCY IS PAPER BACKED BY NOTHING.

—JIM SINCLAIR
MINESET

Since its discovery, every world power has attempted to mine gold all the way out to the farthest reaches of their borders and then some. And when they learned about or found it in the territories of their neighbors, they went to war or simply looted the castle without a fight. Recall the plundering by the Spanish of aboriginal American gold in the late 1500s, resulting in the untimely demise of the Aztecs, Mayas and Incas.

Several millennia after their initial unearthing, gold and silver were recognized as the most valuable monetary units across the globe, with several countries eventually establishing their own gold standard, which set limits on the value of their own currency and the amount of credit that could be issued. As with all good policies, somewhere along the way, those policies became corrupted by the avarice of a few who sought to consolidate the world's gold supply and control and manipulate whatever else lay beyond their reach.

Sterling and Peggy Seagrave have studied all aspects of gold for many years. They summarize their belief about who controls the world's gold:

"I don't like using the word cartel for gold or diamonds, but there is a relatively small group of people who control most of the smelted gold we call LGS for London Gold Standard, because all the members of the network of banks and billionaires/trillionaires like to know the quality/purity/track-record of the gold they handle.

"This network obviously includes the Rothschilds, Rockefellers, Mellons, Morgans, and all the other super-rich who also own chains of banks and control world affairs through a pyramid of gofers including leaders of government, armed forces, and secret services in the public and private sectors, all benefitting from influence peddling.

"Within this network there are certain clusters where they intersect with the Vatican, Masons, the Sicilian Mafia, and countless other underworld groups that also deal in hard drugs—most of the laundered money from which ends up in US banks, with UK banks, Swiss banks, and offshore banks, including the CIA 'black banks' first set up by Paul Helliwell for Wild Bill Donovan and Meyer Lansky in OSS and early CIA days.

"Not everyone who has masses of LGS gold belongs to these networks, like the Chinese who work independently, and the Indian gold jewelry trade, which has its own channels. There is still a great deal of 'Marcos' gold resmelted from what he recovered of Yamashita's Gold, and reburied in several remote stashes guarded by a group known as the Elders.

"And several very rich Filipino families keep their hoards of ingots and biscuit bars in large vaults beneath big buildings in Manila, Cebu, and other cities."

Without question, the control of gold lies in the hands of a very select few, which makes most ordinary people shy away from any thoughts of gold, let alone any ideas of ownership. So why should a short history of gold concern the average American?

Details aside, what should concern you most is how gold has been vaulted from a beautiful aesthetic object to a symbol of absolute power, endless control and abject greed. Gold isn't something you can eat or drink. It's only worth something because we place high value in it. Yes, gold has some very special physico-chemical properties that make it prized, but this doesn't concern the average citizen. Interestingly, gold's physical properties don't even compare to those of carbon nanotubes or graphene.

We wish to possess gold and call it ours, show it off to friends and acquaintances, and visitors from afar. In times of economic strife, gold bought shelter, food and safety to those who had it. For others, it led to an early death at the hand of someone else who coveted the booty and had the means to snatch it.

Truth?

Like any object, gold only has value if people feel it has value and those people express their feelings by paying handsomely for it with some form of money, labor or other instrument of exchange. People the world over feel that gold is the best means of protecting one's personal wealth.

A question for you: what if you were stranded on a deserted island in the middle of the Pacific with no food, and you were offered the choice between ten pounds of gold or ten pounds of McDonald's double quarter-pounders with that rich, golden cheese?

In the US, the Coinage Act of 1873 firmly established the gold standard over silver, the value of which immediately fell sharply. For the next 60 years, gold should have become the buffer that protected the US dollar and, in a perfect world, it would have guaranteed its value.

Unfortunately, the forceful passage of the illegal (i.e. not properly ratified by the requisite number of states) Federal Reserve Act of 1913 by the Jesuits virtually guaranteed that the dollar would never be protected by sufficient reserves of gold, which were—and still are—being leveraged more than 10 to 1 by the Jesuits.

Where is We The People's constitutional and moral protection with this system?

Even worse, the institution of the illegal and unconstitutional US personal income tax in 1913 paved a long and wide road down which the Jesuits drove its chariots of war right up to the doorstep of America, and began a century of rape, murder, plunder and dominance over our once-sovereign nation.

We The People Are Still Comatose

"Banking was conceived in iniquity and was born in sin. The bankers own the earth. Take it away from them, but leave them the power to create money, and with the flick of the pen they will create enough deposits to buy it back again. However, take it away from them, and all the great fortunes like mine will disappear and they ought to disappear, for this would be a happier and better world to live in. But, if you wish to remain the slaves of bankers and pay the cost of your own slavery, let them continue to create money."

—Sir Josiah Stamp
former Director, Bank of England

A t the end of the 19th century, people were beginning to hear what was going on behind the scenes, and were taking a keen interest. It took brave souls to step out in public and onto a soapbox and deliver a moving speech that educated and captivated an audience.

Mrs. Mary Lease was a brilliant orator and ardent campaigner for William Jennings Bryan, a Democrat who ran unsuccessfully for President several times. In her 12 August 1896 speech at Cooper Union Hall, she said:

"An organized effort is making to deceive the people. There are two great enemies of thought and progress, the aristocracy of royalty and the aristocracy of gold. Long ago, the aristocracy of royalty came to a common plane with the common people by the discovery of gunpowder, and the two met on a common field. Where is the respect of old for royalty? Even the English speak of their sovereign, Queen Victoria, as being made not of common clay, but of common mud. The aristocracy of royalty is dying out.

"But here in this country we find in place of an aristocracy of royalty an aristocracy of wealth. Far more dangerous to the race is it than the aristocracy of royalty. It is the aristocracy of gold that disintegrates society, destroys individuals and has ruined the proudest nations. It has called Rothschild's agent here to make the platform of the Republican party."

Fast-forward more than 100 years: that organized effort to deceive We The People is still very much in place. Worst of all, it is so deeply entrenched that we may never wrest ourselves from its deadly grasp.

Interesting, too, that even 100 years ago the common people thought of their Queen as being made of mud. Not much has changed since then, with political parties and their member being harshly questioned and even publicly criticized by their constituents. It's gotten ugly, as We The People have slowly awakened to the fact that their elected representatives are not representing them.

Riots are breaking out in many parts of the US, and we're starting to see the emergence of a new police power: the use of deadly force by law enforcement agencies and the illegal use of military troops.

The Posse Comitatus Act of 1878 strictly forbids the use of any members of the US military as law enforcement officials on non-federal property, although members of the US military have been used to kill Americans in the past. Witness: US Army snipers, TDY (temporary duty) to the CIA, participating in assassinating President John F. Kennedy in 1963; a US Army sniper, TDY to the CIA, killed Dr. Martin Luther King, Jr.; US military operators killed David Koresh and his followers outside Waco, Texas in 1993, and then murdered many federal agents and other innocents who "knew too much." A sad example: the kill list during the Clinton presidency numbers in the dozens and includes many of the Clinton's personal employees and associates.

Why conscript members of We The People's own military?

Because they're already the best-trained men in the business of madness and mayhem, and they naturally love to kill "bad guys" and destroy things. One high-ranking member of an elite US Army special forces unit told me, "I don't care who's in charge, I just follow orders."

There are many more relatively unknown examples of the misuse of our beloved US military on US soil, but you get the picture, yes?

The current Administration avoided the issue of using military forces in a civilian police capacity by signing a secret agreement with Canada on February 14, 2008, The Canada-US Civil Assistance Plan (CAP). The agreement allows Canadian troops to "assist" US law enforcement during civil unrest. The Canadian government also may summon the US military for assistance during similar actions on Canadian soil.

When Canadian armed forces are requested by the US to cross our border, they will be working directly for the US Department of Defense and will be under the command of the US military. Interestingly, the US military may not even be actively participating in the same civil action as the Canadians at that moment. US military authorities could be acting solely as directors of the civil action, in which the Canadians are the sole military supporters of US civilian law enforcement.

US Air Force General Victor Renuart, Commander of the nascent US Northern Command, stated, "This document is a unique, bilateral military plan to align our respective national military plans to respond quickly to the other nation's requests for military support of civil authorities.

"Unity of effort during bilateral support for civil support operations such as floods, forest fires, hurricanes, earthquakes and effects of a terrorist attack, in order to save lives, prevent human suffering and mitigate damage to property, is of the highest importance, and we need to be able to have forces that are flexible and adaptive to support rapid decision-making in a collaborative environment."

To inspect the entire CAP, please turn to the Postscript at the end of this book.

So, not only are We The People comatose, we are being held hostage by the very government that we entrusted with our lives, liberty and the pursuit of a happy and meaningful life.

It's not unlike being in ICU, shackled to a stainless-steel bed, IVs continuously dripping sedatives, hallucinogens and toxins into our bloodstream, while our loved-ones stand hopelessly by and not questioning doctors' orders.

Shame on all of us.

9

Money Out Of Thin Air

"My agency in procuring the passage of the national banking act was the mistake of my life. It has built up a monopoly that affects every interest in the country. It should be repealed. But before this can be accomplished, the people will be arrayed on one side and the banks on the other in a contest such as we have never seen in this country."

–Salmon P. Chase
former Secretary of the Treasury

Shortly before WWII, the Jesuits' agent in the White House, President Franklin D. Roosevelt, abolished the gold standard, thus permitting them to float the US dollar on a cushion of thin foul air, on 19 April 1933.

Printing money of no value became the norm, allowing the Jesuit–owned and controlled Fed to make substantial loans to Americans and their hard-won businesses, without the responsibility of backing the Fed's money with real security. The Jesuits earned astronomical sums from interest paid on those loans, too.

In essence, a dollar was certainly not worth a dollar, but much less and, if one wished to convert that dollar to something of true value, i.e. gold, Americans were now at a total loss. The previous gold standard allowed anyone holding a bank note to exchange that note for real 99.9% gold or, in the case of the silver standard, real 99.9% silver. Our government and its people believed in the value of gold (and silver), and thus used gold as a foundation of the worth of our currency.

Without the so-called gold standard, which by the way has always been controlled by the Jesuits, those very wolves then began calling in all gold. They had Roosevelt make it illegal to own gold under Executive Orders 6102 and 6260. Those who complied reluctantly surrendered their gold for worthless dollars. No one really knows how much gold was confiscated during that time, from April 5, 1933 to 1974, when President Gerald Ford revoked 6260.

The Jesuits devalued the US dollar in 1933, while immediately raising the price of gold from about $20 per ounce to $35 dollars an ounce. Those who turned in their coveted wealth lost the golden opportunity to earn a 75% return on their gold investment.

And those who either kept their gold or bought it at $20 an ounce had nearly doubled their money overnight.

These past few years have seen the same scheme, but on a much larger scale and resulting in much more economic destruction of the American economy. Gold has risen to dizzying heights, fluctuated about in a long, slow teasing fashion to lure in last-minute "investors," and soon will rise again to a level that no ordinary citizen can afford. It creates a false ceiling of hope, all that glittering gold in the sky: so close, yet so far, far away. . . .

We The People will be enticed, then soon forced to sell our gold for what appears to be excellent money. . . .

Money that soon will become *worthless* during a period of hyperinflation and great economic calamity. Why?

The US dollar will be recalled by the Treasury and replaced with a new form of currency, which has already been designed and is now being prepared for formal introduction to the public.

Those who keep their dollars will be left in the cold, along with all that green-colored stocking-stuffer and toilet paper. Those who have physical gold (and silver), however, at least have something with which to exchange goods and services. But there's also a problem there: if you own and trade in gold, someone will find out about you and your gold stash, hunt you down and take your gold, maybe even murder you for it.

You're damned if you possess it, damned if you don't.

10

Is It Gold . . . Or Is It Tungsten?

"*Allegations of missing gold from our Ft. Knox vaults are being widely discussed in European financial circles. But what is puzzling is that the Administration is not hastening to demonstrate conclusively that there is no cause for concern over our gold treasure—if indeed it is in a position to do so.*"

–Edith Roosevelt, granddaughter of Theodore Roosevelt
The New Hampshire Sunday News
9 March 1975

Where did all that confiscated gold go? In 1933, President Roosevelt ordered that We The People turn it in, but as soon as we lost sight of it, we *really* lost sight of it. And so did many of the people who actually took it from us.

It was supposed to be melted down, purified, and then used to forge new gold bullion, which would be stored at the United States Bullion Depository at Ft. Knox, Kentucky, whose gold-storage facility was constructed in 1936. If you believe the statements on the US Mint website, the facility now houses 147.3 million ounces of gold, although its purity is not revealed.

Over the decades, there have been many reports that gold originating from stores at Ft. Knox was not 99.9% gold. Not by far. To start, the majority of Ft. Knox's gold was first smelted from US coinage, the purity of which was about 90%, the balance being made up of copper or other metals to stabilize the coins and make them more durable over time.

These coin-melts also had a slightly different hue than the 99.99% pure gold bullion: they were slightly more orange in color, due to the doping with other metals, especially copper. This fact was painfully evident during the infamous Ft. Knox Tour of 1974 and still echoes today, although faintly, in the chambers of concerned citizens.

At that time, Secretary of Treasury William Simon directed Mary Brooks, Director of the U.S. Mint, to escort select Congressmen and members of the media on a guided tour of some of the vaults at Ft. Knox. The carnival tour, on 23 September 1974, lasted about four hours, and featured only one of the dozen compartments that supposedly contained America's gold reserves, and that compartment was not the main central core, also known as the "Gold Vault."

Those involved in what is now regarded as a cover-up forgot one little detail.

After the tour, some folks remarked about the orange hue of all the 99.9% pure gold bars. With more questions than answers, the house of cards that was a shoddy cover-up began to fall and scatter. In the end, though, nothing new was revealed and with time the whole matter seemed to disappear.

The horror story gets worse: more than 30 years later, Ft. Knox was hit with another scandal, exposed by writer Dan Eden:

"This [gold] bar would feel right in the hand, it would have a dead ring when knocked as gold should, it would test right chemically, it would weigh *exactly* the right amount, and though I don't know this for sure, I think it would also pass an x-ray fluorescence scan, the 1/16" layer of pure gold being enough to stop the x-rays from reaching any tungsten. You'd pretty much have to drill it to find out it's fake."

Allegedly, the Chinese government received nearly 6,000 tungsten-core gold bars in 2009, only to discover upon close inspection that they were all counterfeit. Serial numbers traced the metal bars back to Ft. Knox. The results of China's investigation suggest that there may be as many as 1.5 million 400-ounce tungsten-core gold bars on the worldwide market today, a value of more than $600B.

Billion.

Dollars.

Even though it's long after the fact, it is intriguing to note that, in 2004, NM Rothschilds & Sons, Ltd., the London-based corporation of the Rothschild's investment bank, quietly withdrew from the gold market. What did the Rothschilds know that We The People did not? Was the House of Rothschild making a false ploy? Something to suggest that there was something amiss in the gold market?

Well, it worked: curiously, within four years of withdrawing from the gold market, the value of gold held by the Rothschilds more than doubled.

Previously, the price of gold had been set in exclusive meetings at the offices of NM Rothschilds & Sons, Ltd. in London, at least until they withdrew from the gold market and their seat was taken by Barclays. Twice a day, a small group of five men, connected to each other in a cold virtual reality via conference call, calmly fix the price of gold, a ripple that soon propagates across the world in all gold markets and sets the tone for all gold trading.

Many have asked: why are these particular men setting the price of a commodity that is traded in 165 different countries? Who chose them and how?

London has long been the financial seat of gold trading, and over the centuries has set all gold standards for the world to follow. It would be next to impossible to unseat London as the standards-setting capital for gold in the world.

He who controls the gold makes all the rules, including who controls the gold and what the rules are and who makes them.

All the above machinations have been, and still are, manipulated by the Jesuits through cleverly crafted transnational interactions among their minions within the House of Rothschild. Do you honestly think the Rothschilds actually withdrew from gold trading? No, they are still the Jesuits' accountants, and are actively manipulating the entire gold market, while deceiving the world into thinking they have retreated into their lair.

Clever tactics and strategies, indeed. But no longer transparent.

11

Another Insider Blows The Whistle

Federal Reserve notes are not redeemable in gold, silver or any other commodity, and receive no backing by anything. This has been the case since 1933. The notes have no value for themselves, but for what they will buy. In another sense, because they are legal tender, Federal Reserve notes are "backed" by all the goods and services in the economy.

Statement of the United States Treasury

Are there any historical precedents that signal what economic disaster may be coming? As stated previously, yes. If you correlate the price of gold with the state of the economy in the US over the past 65 years, you see that when gold rises steeply, the dollar is somehow devalued, leading to extreme economic instability. In short, a prolonged recession or even a depression from which it takes decades to recover. All of this is well orchestrated, of course, by the Jesuits.

Over the past 12 years, in particular, there have been many indicators of manipulation of economic markets, especially gold. So much so that formal groups and companies have formed to study the situation, to provide countermeasures. The Gold Anti-Trust Action Committee (GATA), chaired by Mr. Bill Murphy, was founded by Mr. Murphy and Mr. Chris Powell. Mr. Murphy explained:

"We'd heard that Long-Term Capital Management was short 400 tons of gold. We figured when they blew up, they would have to cover their position. JP Morgan, Deutsche Bank, Chase Manhattan all were selling when gold got around $300. Then I heard some other things and I said, this is being managed here. One thing led to another and we started GATA in January of 1999. I was on CNBC the next two weeks and that was the last time I'd been heard in America. I've been blackballed ever since. Not even our name [GATA] mentioned."

"Why did they [House of Rothschild] get out of the gold-fixing business? They knew this was going to blow up and they're very very smart people. I think they knew it was sort of a Ponzi scheme, and the gold market was going to blow up and they didn't want to be around it."

"We at GATA have put together 12 years of evidence and so we know what's happening. Things are beginning to blow up. We are now suing the Fed because we've uncovered some talk about gold swaps and we used the Freedom of Information Act to have them tell us what was going on. They refused to tell us anything, saying these are secrets so they didn't have to tell."

"[Two years] ago, European central banks stopped selling gold to the general public."

"The Gold Cartel is running out of available central bank gold to meet the burgeoning demand."

Ironically and not surprisingly, The Gold Cartel also is selling more gold stock than ever before, despite the paucity of the very product that should back each stock transaction.

"We presented testimony at the Commodity Futures Trade Commission, the CFTC, hearings on March 25, 2010 and dropped a bomb on them: a former JP Morgan trader told everyone how JP Morgan was making money flushing out speculators.

"They were making money when everyone else was obviously losing money, so they were laughing at the rest of the world.

"The whistleblower, Andrew Maguire, and his wife were hit by a car the next day outside of London. The motorist hit two more cars, and there was a helicopter chase before they caught him. Not one word about the guy who hit them has been made. Not one word since. It was another coincidence arising from this hearing: first, the live webcast feed of my testimony went dark during the entire testimony, then Andrew gets hit by a car. Again, just a coincidence?"

"This story went viral on the Internet in China, Russia, across the world, but not here in the United States until the *Post's* story."

After nearly 12 years of media silence on GATA, the *New York Post*, on Sunday, 11 April 2010, published a story by Michael Gray, "Metal$ are in the pits: Trader blows whistle on gold & silver price manipulation," describing for the first time in more than a decade the price manipulation of gold and silver on the open market.

"JP Morgan acts as an agent for the Federal Reserve; they act to halt the rise of gold and silver against the US dollar. JP Morgan is insulated from potential losses [on their short positions] by the Fed and/or the US taxpayer. HSBC conducts an ongoing manipulative concentrated naked short position in gold. Silver is much easier to manipulate due to its much smaller [market] size," Maguire said.

At the same CFTC hearing, one man said that there is 50 times more gold traded than is available physically, but then Mr. Jeff Christian of the commodities firm CPM Group corrected this statistic on the record. He said that the London Bullion Market Association (LBMA) leverages gold 100 to one, meaning that if, at any one time, 100 people demand their physical gold bullion be given to them, only one customer's request could be granted. The other 99 customers would have to settle for cash, its price determined by the exchange.

"That is tantamount to a default on the trade," says Murphy.

In that same *Post* article, Andrew Maguire stated boldly: "If you sell something you do not own, then that is fraud."

The Jesuits and their accountants, the House of Rothschild, have committed fraud against We The People for more than 200 hundred years. Isn't it time We The People stood up against the demons in Rome?

12

What Can We The People Really Do?

The Federal Reserve definitely caused the Great Depression by contracting the amount of currency in circulation by one-third from 1929 to 1933.

— Milton Friedman
Nobel Laureate in Economics

My Dear Reader, the bankers within our own walls have been in charge far too long, aiding the House of Rothschild and its higher authority, the Jesuits in Rome. And they've ridden roughshod over us in the most evil of ways, something they've done since 1541.

Truth be told, what we're seeing in 2014 isn't anything new; it's just happening at an accelerated pace, due to the potential ability of We The People to amass a resistance quickly.

Our ancestors had to put up with the same load of manure, too. Unfortunately for them, they lacked the modern communications tools we have today, those very tools that pose such a threat to the Jesuits and their global plan for We The People: cell phones, Worldwide Web, email, satellite phones, Skype, Twitter, Facebook, etc.

Even with these tools, Americans and ordinary citizens the world over are still in the dark about the machinations of the Jesuits and their minions. A touch of irony here: the good people in the rural areas of Afghanistan communicate better than we Westerners do, and they do it surprisingly efficiently via word of mouth.

Over the past 65 years alone, the Jesuits have engaged in numerous gold scandals that, even today, have not been fully investigated, let alone revealed:

- The theft, concealment, storage, and distribution of Japan's gold, looted from various Asian countries
- The Bank of England's transfer of Czech gold reserves to the Nazis was orchestrated by US lawyer and soon-to-be Secretary of State John Foster Dulles and his law firm, Sullivan and Cromwell
- Surreptitiously escorting Martin Bormann, Hitler's private secretary and head of the Nazi Party Chancellery, not to mention a Jesuit-installed agent, out of Germany on the final night and day of the war so the Allies (read: the Jesuits) could recover the Nazi's gold and wealth, stolen from victims and secreted into Swiss bank accounts and vaults. The Allies resmelted most of the Nazi gold, although because of "poor record keeping," an accurate accounting may never be known to We The People.

These are just a few examples of known transgressions by the Jesuits. There are hundreds more that await our discovery and clinical inspection.

The Seagraves offer a rather bleak commentary on our times:

"Most Americans have no idea what's going on and don't care, so long as they are entertained and fed. America is now the biggest trouble maker in the world, Israel second. Nobody faces up to reality if they can find a way to slide around it. Everyone should have a gold nest egg (Maple Leaves, Krugerrands, etc.) salted away, but it would be stupid to put it in a bank."

So why must the second gold rush matter to you, my dear fellow Americans?

Because it signals the beginning of the end of our beloved dollar, which, as the Seagraves stated, "is toilet paper and until there is a new global currency, the scammers who play the money and commodity markets will be jacking rates up and down to enrich themselves even further. Look at Goldman Sachs gaming away."

In short, we're not in the "Great Recession" stated blithely on every Jesuit-owned TV network. We are now in a major depression in the United States, quite unlike anything this country has ever seen, and it will take us years to recover. If we rely on the historical record of the Jesuits to guide us, we can also expect another major war, which will probably be started by Israel and/or the US against Iran and her Arab neighbors.

Closer to home, we will see more restrictive legislation along the lines of the Patriot Act of 2001 and the Homeland Security Act of 2002 that further dismantles and wrecks our beloved Constitution and thus our rights as American citizens.

You might recall the impressive Patriot Act, which weighed in at a whopping 132 pages, not including all the supporting materials, and was allegedly in response to the staged 9/11 attacks, which had occurred only a month before. If you read the Act, you'll be struck by its extreme detail, thoughtfulness, and thoroughness, an action that clearly took much longer than a month to research, design, write, discuss among members of Congress, pass and finally implement. All those actions were performed by our US government and took just over one month?

Really now?

Here's the accurate truth:

This bill had been prepared several years in advance of the 9/11 attacks. Considering how long it has taken to research, write and debate the healthcare bill of 2010—several years—it is highly unlikely that our own government was capable in any way of establishing the Patriot Act in one month, in response to false-flag attacks on American soil on 11 September 2001.

And who would be charged with covering up or disseminating false and misleading information about all this mess? BigMedia, which is owned and controlled by the Jesuits, will continue to issue false and misleading information about the plots and intrigues of the powers that be, while also withholding important knowledge and details about these machinations.

Savvy and frustrated Americans are turning to alternative media, much of it underground and well off the radar. The financial gurus in this country are banding together and airing their grievances, thoughts, ideas, hypotheses and theories about what is happening today. Other sectors are slower to react, but we see more and more people in business, engineering, medicine and science migrating to non-mainstream media sources. They trickle in a few a day, but that trickle will soon lead to a flood as good people begin to educate themselves about the ill deeds of the Jesuits.

Not surprisingly, the Jesuits have caught on to this wave of dissension in the ranks and has established its own controlled opposition, i.e. fake news and information sites that purport to support the common man and woman.

One of these is Newsmax.com, a slick "news outlet" run by a man who just happens to elbows with low-ranking members of the Jesuits, those who give him his marching orders, and he then packages them in a series of dolled-up newsletters and websites. FoxNews and CNN, too, spit out the same disinformation that feeds Americans' thirsty minds, cleverly mixing just enough fact with lavish fiction.

Fareed Zakaria, Glenn Beck and even so-called "conspiracy theorists" like Jesse Ventura and Alex Jones, too, are owned and controlled by the Jesuits, spouting out mountains of half-truths that lure people in, making the good We The People feel wanted, needed and cared for by someone who has the power to carry our grievances to the highest authority.

Like there's some big brother out there looking out for our best interests.

Well, there is a Big Brother out there. And he does care about us, he cares to soften us up to a malleable consistency, a point where we no longer even think about, let alone counter, the dangers around us.

These so-called "conspiracy theorists" I listed above are actually "false opposition," i.e. fake conspiracy theorists who, again, are employed and controlled by the Jesuits as a means to corral and then ultimately control We The People. Zakaria in particular is very effective because he's so spit-shined and well spoken, and he has a world-class venue from which to pontificate "his" views, which are widely circulated to a very gullible worldwide public.

In short, all this false opposition is so nipped up and tarty that no hot-blooded American could possible resist.

Pulling in We The People in this way is like taking a big, fat magnet and applying it to a pile of iron shavings. Do it yourself, see how the shavings react.

Magnetism is one of the most powerful forces in the Universe. . . .

13

And Now, Behold The Great Collapse

"The object of every trust in this country is to manufacture debts on the industrial resources of this country. Those men do not go into business to make money out of the industry itself."

—T. Cushing Daniel
Testifying to the US Senate Committee
on Interstate Commerce
10 January 1912

In what Mr. John Williams of Shadow Government Statistics terms "The Great Collapse," one of the consequences of very high gold prices, among other economic indicators, is a steep fall from grace:

"The U.S. economic and systemic solvency crises of the last two years are just precursors to a Great Collapse: a hyperinflationary great depression. Such will reflect a complete collapse in the purchasing power of the U.S. dollar, a collapse in the normal stream of U.S. commercial and economic activity, a collapse in the U.S. financial system as we know it, and a likely realignment of the U.S. political environment.

"The current U.S. financial markets, financial system and economy remain highly unstable and vulnerable to unexpected shocks. The Federal Reserve is dedicated to preventing deflation, to debasing the U.S. dollar. The results of those efforts are being seen in tentative selling pressures against the U.S. currency and in the rallying price of gold."

Further support by Mr. Williams for the belief that deliberate government actions are amplifying the current depression:

"In the midst of the crises, the Obama Administration has introduced major new government programs, ranging from carbon tax plans to a national health care and insurance program. Irrespective of any stated goals of not increasing the federal deficit further, these programs will have severely negative impact on the federal deficit, either from massive net expenses, or from losses in tax revenues in a weaker economy."

Hyperinflation is definitely on its way, and instead of coming in 2018, as predicted by some, it'll be here earlier:

"The intensifying economic and solvency crises, and the responses to both by the U.S. government and the Federal Reserve in the last two years, have exacerbated the government's solvency issues and moved forward my timing estimation for the hyperinflation to the next five years, from the 2010 to 2018 timing range estimated in the prior report.

"The U.S. government and Federal Reserve already have committed the system to this course through the easy politics of a bottomless pocketbook, the servicing of big-moneyed special interests, gross mismanagement, and a deliberate and ongoing effort to debase the U.S. currency. Accordingly, risks are particularly high of the hyperinflation crisis breaking within the next year."

Here's a metric of the bad times to come: when the Fed exercises more and more "quantitative easing," you know undoubtedly that they're manipulating the market for the worse and We The People will be the ones to suffer.

Quantitative easing, in case you were not familiar with the term, means that the Jesuit-owned Federal Reserve seeks to "balance out" the negative effects of a recession or depression by injecting substantial money, which was created out of thin air, into our economy, as it did in the late 1920s, thus causing further inflation then hyperinflation.

Money that will soon become worthless, much like the trillion-mark notes of the Weimar Republic nearly 90 years ago.

When enough of We The People have been lured in by surprisingly easy credit, more loans and second and third mortgages at low interest rates, the Jesuits' accountants then severely contract the money supply, and call in those loans and mortgages.

The result of this quantitative easing? First, few people can afford to pay off those loans and mortgages, so they lose the very thing they were trying to protect: businesses, jobs, homes, real estate, and personal property.

The whole scenario soon descends into a great depression.

It's happened many times before, and not just in the US, and it's happening again. Right now under We The People's noses.

Mr. Williams shares a few important criteria, all further indicators of the Romanic depression:

"Prerequisites to the crisis unfolding include: Federal Reserve moving to monetize U.S. Treasury debt; U.S. dollar losing its traditional safe-haven status; U.S. dollar losing its reserve status; Federal budget deficit and Treasury funding needs spiraling out of control.

"The Fed moved to monetize Treasury debt in November 2010. A much-diminished U.S. dollar safe-haven status has become evident in early March 2011, along with serious calls for a new global reserve currency. The economy is not in recovery and should display significant new weakness in the months ahead, with severely expansive implications for the federal deficit, Treasury funding needs a requisite Fed monetization of debt."

All the criteria are in place for The Great Collapse that is ramping up now and last for years, with the aftermath being much worse and longer-lasting than what we're seeing in the current atmosphere.

Other than educating ourselves with the accurate truth, what can We The People do to protect ourselves?

14

Why Should We The People Care?

William Pitt, who was one of the greatest men England ever produced, was chancellor of the exchequer of England. The Government being in great need of supplies, they approached the Bank of England, which was a close corporation, a private enterprise with which the English Government had nothing in the world to do. The bank, represented mostly at that time by the Rothschilds, stated to Pitt that if he would allow them to issue notes upon a Government debt to the extent of £3,000,000, they would loan him that amount of money for five years without interest and that they should have the privilege of issuing the bank's notes against that public debt. That was the beginning of this idea of issuing a public debt and predicating credit money on it. Subsequently, realizing his mistake, William Pitt . . . said of the inauguration of the first national bank in the United States, under Alexander Hamilton: 'Let the American people go into their debt-funding schemes and banking systems, and from that hour their boasted independence will be a mere phantom.'

—T. Cushing Daniel
Testifying to the US Senate Committee
on Interstate Commerce
10 January 1912

It's been 10 years since the House of Rothschild was directed by the Jesuits to pull out of gold-fixing, a position they had held and an industry they had controlled for more than 100 years. But please don't be fooled: they still control it via their own agents sitting on the board. Their having pulled out was merely another ploy.

Interestingly, the gold market has been in a downturn, trading at a high of $1,909.30 an ounce on Aug. 23, 2011, declining steadily over the ensuing months, then fluctuating about the $1,300 mark as of mid-2014.

In past markets when the price of gold rose more than 50% in a short time, the overall economy nose-dived into a recession or, even worse, a depression. These aren't simply the beginnings of a depression, we've been in one for several years, and are headed toward collapse of our once-strong infrastructure:

- Skyrocketing gold prices (silver will soon follow)
- High inflation approaching hyperinflation
- Poor housing market with runaway foreclosures and seizures
- High unemployment, with greater numbers of illegal aliens crossing the border to work and attend schools and colleges in the US
- Severe increase in personal income taxes, which do not get re-invested in the US
- Clear and present destruction of essential means of communication among We The People: the US Postal Service and the Internet
- Restricted air and land travel, now monitored and enforced by TSA
- General public lethargy and severe ignorance about these important affairs

The very people who designed and built this system of gold trading, wrote all the legislation that governs it, made all the rules for trading, are in a unique position: they can manipulate it at will, anytime, anywhere, and without permission from anyone. And they're doing it right now.

Even if you don't care about gold or the gold market, this gloomy situation should matter to you. It should matter because if gold continues to rise or at least hover at a high point for some time, and all the other criteria described above continue in place, then you and your family will be in the middle of the worst depression in the history of the world.

Here's the worst news for you: we're deep in that depression right now. Don't be fooled by BigMedia telling you it's only a recession. They're lying. The greatest transfer of wealth is happening as you watch your favorite TV show or movie, indulge in that pint of Ben & Jerry's, vacation in Yellowstone.

This dire situation should matter to you because the Jesuits have stolen your hard-earned money right from under you, taken your wonderful home, driven you to bankruptcy, and pushed some of you out the window. Literally.

Regardless of whether you have the funds to buy pounds and pounds of gold bullion, you can buy gold in small quantities. And if you can't afford gold, buy silver. Historically, both gold and silver have rebounded after crashes, only to rise up again in the next cycle of price fixing and manipulation by The First Sphere of Influence.

GATA's Bill Murphy said, "Understanding that the manipulation of the price of gold is profoundly important to all markets and the American public. On January 31, 2008, GATA placed a $264,000 full-page color advertisement in *The Wall Street Journal*. GATA's ad warned, 'This manipulation has been a primary cause of the catastrophic excesses in the markets that now threaten the whole world.' What GATA warned against has come to pass."

Let's once again address the salient question from the previous chapter: What can We The People do?

As with all other coming disasters, educate yourself first about the dangers, both overt and hidden. With a little knowledge, you may save yourself and your family.

Sadly, it won't do much good to talk with your so-called elected officials like Congressmen and Senators, because they're part of the grand scheme that is destroying America today, part of the great inside job that is clandestinely eating away at the very fabric of our existence and the foundation of our country.

They are traitors to us all.

When we have a sitting president signing international agreements that strip us of our Constitutional rights, increasing taxes on the moderately wealthy (not the super rich, mind you), and pursuing a fascist policy on behalf of the Jesuits, then we know we're in deep trouble and must act decisively, and do so en masse.

We The People can only act collectively. Individuals who blow whistles at their place of work are summarily dismissed or, worse, murdered for what they knew and tried to expose. But a large group of citizens is tough to corral, let alone murder.

Bill Murphy adds:

"If this [current] trend continues, we could see gold at $3000 to $5000 an ounce. And with hyperinflation, much higher than that."

"Gold is a barometer (thermometer) of US financial market health. The Gold Cartel defused this barometer by suppressing the price of gold, which aided the Fed in keeping interest rates too low, for too long. This led directly to the financial market and economic debacles of the day.

"After all, what does the press talk about when the price of gold soars: too much inflation, a US dollar problem, or a crisis of some other sort. All of it is bad for an incumbent administration and Wall Street. Both hate a rising gold price. It is widely mentioned that if gold had kept pace with inflation in the US, it would be $2,300 per ounce. Today it's around [$1,320]. That is how much The Gold Cartel has suppressed the price."

Mr. John Williams' *Shadow Government Statistics* website shows what we feel are real-world economic statistics, stripped of the government and the Jesuits' public-relations spin. In one article, Mr. Williams stated that the true inflation-adjusted price of gold should now be more than $6,000 an ounce.

Most cannot afford to buy gold now, let alone at $6,000 an ounce, so the best plan is for you is to hold on to any gold, silver, platinum and precious metals and gems, and do not be tempted to sell them to the gold buyers that have sprung up on many a corner in Small Town, USA. These gold buyers are tied into a vast network that feeds its bounty up up up the ladder to the Jesuits and their accountants.

In 1933, President Roosevelt ordered that all gold in the hands of citizens be turned in or confiscated.

Should the current Administration even attempt to force We The People to turn over their gold and precious metals, resist at all cost. Don't share with anyone what you have in your safe or vault or safe-deposit box down at the bank. The best security is anonymity.

Again, if you can, buy small amounts of gold and silver and exotic metals like platinum. No one talks about platinum because it's a controlled metal, mostly used in the aerospace and high-tech industries. If you have platinum, keep it. And keep it hidden, along with all the other precious metals you manage to buy and hold.

We The People have immense power over the Jesuits, and those in power do not want us to know this fact. It would take so little on the part of all good citizens to resist the destructive machinations of these demons. The first step is to educate We The People about this destructive force, then suggest important options to oppose and even defeat the Jesuits:

1. Hold on to your gold, silver and exotic metals and gems, and do not tell *anyone* of your holdings or where they're stashed. *The best security is anonymity.*

2. If you own gold stocks or certificates, cash them in immediately and demand physical gold, and have it all independently inspected for purity. When you buy advertised 99.9% pure gold, ensure you receive 99.9% pure gold for your hard-earned money.

3. Do not sell your home. The housing market, or some semblance of it, will bounce back in a few years, when this cycle of destruction passes. If you own land, keep it. Buy even more land, if possible, especially farmland that still yields good crops. Note that there is no such thing as *allodial property* anywhere in the world. The Jesuits claim ownership of all the land and seas; that's why you pay property taxes. Nonetheless, at least We The People get some semblance of "property" to call our own.

4. Cut back on or eliminate all unnecessary spending.

5. Pay off all bills and become debt free.

6. Share expenses with family, friends, neighbors and colleagues.

7. Car pool, use public transportation, or ride a bicycle.

8. Have at least 18 months' worth of dry food supplies, water and any necessary items for emergencies, including gasoline, motor oil and propane.

9. If you live near or on the coast or an area that is considered a danger zone, have an emergency evacuation plan, because we will be seeing a greater number and intensity of storms, hurricanes, tornadoes, floods, droughts, etc.

10. Beware that when the US experiences hyperinflation, the dollar in its present physical form will become worthless. Be prepared to barter with those in your neighborhood, town, city. You will have to set up a bartering network that accepts a new form of "money," and it may be little things like your wedding ring, the shirt off your back, a six-pack of Bud Light, a chain saw, etc.

11. If at all possible, have an emergency plan that allows you to move into the wilderness, especially near a good source of clean, flowing water. A couple of good camping tents, each capable of holding six people, is a good start, plus the typical camping supplies.

12. Buy firearms: at least ten .45-cal pistols and at least 10,000 rounds of .45 ACP Hydra-Shok, or similar defensive hollow-point bullets; five defensive shotguns that fit your body type and size, environment and shooting style, with at least 5,000 rounds of ammunition for close quarters and distance, i.e. about 10 yards away. The plain fact We The People have the power and right to own firearms is written in our Constitution's amendments: Amendment 2 - Right to Bear Arms. Ratified 12/15/1791. "A well regulated Militia, being necessary to the security of a free State, the right of the People to keep and bear Arms, shall not be infringed." Yes, I have stated that our Constitution is a dead letter, but the Jesuits still create the illusion that it still carries its full power, so take advantage of the Jesuits' own ruse and buy weapons and ammo.

13. Remove your deposits from banks and demand cash. With this cash, immediately buy gold and silver. Always buy silver along with gold. The former is typically 95% cheaper and remains the only precious metal whose price has risen higher and faster than gold over the same period of time, despite being demonetized by the Jesuits. Interestingly, it would take only about 10% of a bank's depositors to ruin it if they withdrew their deposits. Banks just do not have enough cash on hand to meet this type of demand, and would most likely close its doors and have armed guards, backed up by the US military, standing outside to keep out We The People.

14. [Note: the following recommendation was written on 8 July, 2014. It may not be accurate when this edition of this book is published, so I urge caution.] For those who afford to, convert 50% of your remaining dollars to gold and silver. Do not tell anyone of your plans/actions. Anonymity is the best security. When gold becomes scarce, silver will be in demand and its price will skyrocket, thus keeping it out of your reach. Eventually, all existing currencies will fall, but this is not likely for the next few years. The Jesuits time their actions based on two main factors: 1. celestial/solar/lunar cycles and 2. The collective behavior of We The People. If there is a severe backlash from We The People, the Jesuits will back down to some extent and not implement their plan to eliminate the US dollar altogether. If We The People acquiesce to their actions, then expect them even to accelerate their machinations.

15. Get a US passport and passport card immediately. They're both available from the US State Department and can be ordered online. If you had to leave the country, you could only do so legally with your passport. The card is for entering the US from Canada, Mexico, Bermuda and the Caribbean. It is not valid for international flight travel. If you're willing to pay the extra $60, you can even get a passport overnighted to you. Passport cards cannot be overnighted, though. Please buy both and keep them with you at all times. Note that the Card has an RFID (radio-frequency identification) chip embedded in it, containing your identifying information. It can be scanned at a distance of approximately 10 feet, depending on the power of the RFID scanner or detector.

16. Move to Cost Rica. Central and South America have largely been brought under the rule of the Jesuits, so they now remain more or less stable, unlike the US, which is undergoing its final slaughter. There is no military there (Costa Rica), and the country is stable economically and socially. Housing is half the normal price of housing in Florida, as of July 2014, and the surrounding areas are much nicer than in Florida. Plus, the most important part of all, are We The People of Costa Rica. Wonderful, sweet, kind, giving, accepting. Welcome to your new home, America. . . .

Many people who have been trained by BigMedia to act and react in certain ways, conduct their lives according to someone else's rules, will not believe the facts in this book. This happens all the time. And when it's too late, those very people are left scratching their heads, wondering what just hit them.

So what do *you* believe?

In whose words and deed, however nicely they're dressed and presented, should you place your trust?

The first item on your agenda, Dear Reader, is simple: educate yourself first with alternative news and views about this subject, news you won't find on mainstream news sites, newspapers, magazines, tv shows, etc. Do as other brave people have done and connect the dots. You will be guided by your own good intuition, so trust your gut. Talk with other like-minded people who share your concerns, trade references and sources of good information, continue researching and disseminating the intelligence you gather.

Allow others to critique your findings, develop hypotheses and theories about the true and accurate history of America, and how we got to this very spot we're in right now.

When We The People take an active role in determining our future direction and progress, without putting it in the hands of evils like the Jesuits and the House of Rothschild, we will rekindle that age-old flame that was so bravely lit by the original Protestant founders of our great country. When we see its multicolored display, feel its warmth, and touch its strength, we will experience as they did: true freedom and the clean atmosphere in which to exercise liberty.

15

Please Don't Shoot The Messenger!

The greatest economic loss I know of that the world has been subjected to is in going down into the bowels of the earth and getting out the precious metals and storing them in vaults, where they never see the light of day. The only justification of it is the fallacy that it is the standard of value.

—T. Cushing Daniel
Testifying to the US Senate Committee
on Interstate Commerce
10 January 1912

Throughout history, the messenger of bad news has usually been the first casualty. Worse, the second casualty has been the news itself. If your aim is to understand what happens behind the scenes of our US government, you must embrace some new information that will be difficult to accept, let alone assimilate.

Please keep an open mind, discard and abandon previous knowledge that was force-fed to you in grade school, high school and college, be willing to consider new and important information, and also take the time from your hectic day—time you don't have—and connect all the dots of circumstantial evidence you discover in your journey to enlightenment.

When you're sufficiently full and well armed, please share your knowledge with others in a very kind, patient, open and accurate way.

Doubtless, you're considering where you could possibly find the time to do anything other than what you normally do in your daily life. Who has time to think about the Jesuits, let alone read an article or book on them and their evil deeds over hundreds of years?

It takes about 15 hours to get through the average 350-page book. Sitting under an umbrella or wading in the gentle surf on vacation for two weeks a year may be the best and only time you have to read, so would you really want to invest two and a half days of your hard-earned time to pore over 100,000 words that will only depress you beneath the sparkling waters of your bliss?

Do you really want to abandon all you know about history and life, and adopt a whole new way of thinking, one that will pit you against the largest and most powerful government on the planet, not to mention the much larger and darker force above it that rules all of humanity?

Are you sure you want to gamble away your life and the lives of your family to fight a force that's been building and plotting against We The People and our fellow citizens of the world for many hundreds of years?

America, we have been programmed to love all that BigMedia have dished out in every size and shape and flavor imaginable, all conveniently available, like a Las Vegas vacation, 24/7/365: ESPN, CNN, FoxNews, Glenn Beck, Oprah, Playboy Channel, HBO, plus the myriad distractions in the form of toys, designer clothes, perfume, makeup, shoes, hot cars, fast boats, sexy women, thrill rides, exotic shows and, oh, so much more!

Step right up, America and get your fix.

We are comfortably numbed by BigMedia, on a lifelong buzz that needs no toke or shot or needle. It's all easy accessible and in such abundance that we're absolutely overwhelmed with all that choice, all those empty calories of noise and nonsense.

This is exactly the state the Jesuits wish for the average American: more pliant, malleable, naïve, ignorant, passive, apathetic, and just plain unresponsive to any ill deeds done to us.

Like boiling a frog slowly, the Jesuits have reduced We The People to a dead, pulpy mass, no longer able to resist on any level, let alone take its last breath.

And all the while, they are removing our Constitutional rights and freedom and liberty, separating us from our hard-earned money, taxing us into bankruptcy and suicide, kicking us out of our homes, and stripping us of any sense of dignity remaining after such wholesale liquidation.

All in the name of world domination.

What can you do to stop this senseless onslaught, Dear Reader?

As stated in the previous chapter, the first steps to changing anything are becoming aware of the subject, then educating yourself as much and as accurately as possible. You're going to need a sizable store of munitions for the coming fight, because it's going to be a long and lonely struggle, with few if any rewards at the finish of your life.

I heartily suggest you take full advantage of your right to bear arms and defend you, your family and your property at all costs, especially if you have physical gold on your property and they know about it.

I've always believed that the best security is anonymity. Don't tell anyone you have your gold, silver or exotic metals. Not even dear friends or neighbors. In the collapse of the Weimar Republic in the early 1920s, neighbors ratted out fellow neighbors for a mere loaf of bread. And in Nazi Germany, "good neighbors" spied on their friends for much less. . . .

During the worst of times, only your dear family is to be trusted with the most sensitive of your personal information. Even then, beware: the Jesuits had the Hitler Youth that exposed even their own parents.

Can you say Boy Scouts, Girl Scouts, church and civic youth groups? The Nazi regime employed youth groups like these to spy on their parents, friends and neighbors, and to report all "suspicious activity" to their Nazi handlers.

All things considered, and the list is quite long, the best you can hope for is make a small contribution to humanity's uphill fight, with the hope and wish that someone in the future will, with your kind benefaction in mind, body and soul, somehow carry on bravely and end up defeating the Jesuits and the House of Rothschild.

The alternative, of course, is to design and build a whole new model that usurps the deadlight of these demons.

16

They Really Own Your Gold, America

Before the printing-press had become of great force, before the public school and the general education of the people had become powerful, there had developed in Europe an "imperial Government" claiming to govern its subjects, the people, "by divine right." These Governments were headed by the Hohenzollerns, the Hapsburgs, the Romanoffs, the Bourbons (Autocracies), who swore in the Secret Treaty of Verona a covenant of hostility to all representative governments (Democracies) and against the education of the people and the freedom of the press.

— Robert Latham Owen
in *Where Is God In The European War?*

wo items are abundantly clear when we think of money and gold over the past two thousand years: 1. Both are manipulated by the Jesuits; and 2. The degree to which the Jesuits have manipulated, and the methods used to manipulate, money and gold have largely been consistent.

After rising from the grave, dusting himself off, and then carefully examining all the machinations of the Jesuits, the great Sun Tzu might offer the following:

"Using the same methods over and over against your enemies is careless and arrogant. It invites not only microscopic scrutiny of your methods, but also the means to counter them effectively. As if it weren't obvious, subsequent generations will surely catch on to you and your simple tactics and strategies, not to mention your hubris. And when your enemy catches up to your shenanigans, you will quickly become toast, your ashes then scattered to the four corners of the earth and then forgotten . . . except by the flowers, vegetables and bugs who feast on your remains and then rise gently and purposefully into a new sunlight."

How To Commandeer A Country Without Anyone Noticing

For the past 235 years, the Jesuits and the House of Rothschild have seized control over a government by first sending in its own spies to infiltrate that government at its highest levels, then establishing a central bank that controls the entire economy of that country. The central bank is a private bank, not unlike Wells Fargo or Bank of America, owned by the Jesuits and operated by the House of Rothschild.

With a central bank in place, the Jesuits then use their power to ride the cycles of celestial, solar and lunar bodies and exacerbate those cycles to the benefit of the Jesuits. In short, while they do not necessarily create depressions and recessions, they know the time and place to light the spark that flames the inevitable fire. The Universe's heavenly bodies work their own gravitational and electromagnetic magic upon earth and her geophysical and living elements, so we are their mercy when we enter a down cycle.

The immediate result is that the government immediately goes into debt, as it must now borrow money from the Jesuits via its newly installed central bank, instead of printing its own money. The interest on those loans is guaranteed by personal income taxes on the people of that country.

Before the systemic invasion by the Jesuits, that country printed its own money that was free of any interest, free of any debt and, therefore, it was not obligated or forced to accept any loans from outside sources, let alone usurious private banks.

As long as people saw their government as legitimate and they respected the government-issued money, the government was in good standing to continue printing and issuing it to its citizens free of any and all debt obligations.

And what happens to that government when it rejects the Jesuits' "offer" to install a private central bank, grant loans to the government, and then have the central bank print debt notes at high interest, plus exact a personal income tax on all citizens of that country?

Simple: the president of that country is assassinated, the Jesuits install a malleable "president," and then proceed on schedule, thus implanting the central bank, forcing the government to take out loans at high interest, forcing that countries citizens to pay a hefty personal income tax to pay the usurious interest on those government loans.

Are there any real-world examples of the above scenario?

Too many to list here.

Please consider the following, all occurring in the US within the last 235 years:

The Revolutionary War: A Continuing War of Independence

The House of Rothschild, under the direction of the Jesuits, sent one of their agents, Alexander Hamilton, to America to whip up sentiment for the country's first central bank. The arguments in favor of such a bank won over many influential people including George Washington.

Thomas Jefferson, though, saw through the dark veil and immediately sought the counsel of Secretary of Treasury, Albert Gallatin. In one of his letters to Gallatin, Jefferson lamented:

"That [Bank of the United States] is so hostile we know: 1. from a knowledge of the principles of the persons composing the body of directors in every bank, principal or branch, and those of most of the stock-holders; 2. from their opposition to the measures and principles of the government and to the election of those friendly to them; and, 3. from the sentiments of the newspapers they support.

"Now, while we are strong, it is the greatest duty we owe to the safety of our Constitution to bring this powerful enemy to a perfect subordination under its authorities....

"I pray you to turn this subject in your mind and give it the benefit of your knowledge of details; whereas, I have only very general views of the subject."

The First Bank of the United States was established by Congress on February 25, 1791, the day America plunged into debt by having to accept loans from the Jesuits at usurious interest, with the design that they could never be repaid.

Interestingly, our Founding Fathers knew exactly who the Jesuits were, and our brave and courageous Fathers spoke and wrote about them, mostly privately. It is a shame, though, that our Fathers dropped the sword in the final hour and ceased fighting the Jesuits in our Fathers' golden years. Perhaps they delegated duties to the next generation? The results show abject failure, so one can only speculate. We do know that Thomas Paine traveled to France to stir up anti-Jesuit sentiment and, sometime soon after, the world witnessed the French Revolution. Cause and effect? It's also been hypothesized that Paine himself was a Jesuit who manipulated those in the highest sectors of government. Who really knows?

The War of 1812

Over the next 20 years, as America fell deeper into debt, many original supporters of the Bank dropped from its ranks and voiced concern over the true nature of this private central bank, owned and controlled by a group of men in Rome with operations in London. It appeared to the new dissenters that America had not, in fact, won the War of Independence at all. Quite the opposite: the United States was now firmly in the iron grasp of England (Rome) more than ever.

When the First Bank's charter was not renewed by the US in 1811, the Jesuits ordered Nathan Mayer Rothschild to punish the Americans. Hence, the War of 1812 during which the Jesuit-controlled British army, on August 24, 1814, destroyed both the White House and Capitol, among other government buildings. Two years later, President James Madison capitulated, and the Second Bank of the United States was established, thus frustrating the US's continual attempts to dislodge the poisonous roots of the House of Rothschild from American soil.

"Old Hickory" Routs Out The House Of Rothschild

President Andrew Jackson's primary goal was to expose the Jesuits and the House of Rothschild to We The People, then remove them from our lands. His famous spirited indictment of these foreign bankers still echoes well: "I have read the scriptures, gentlemen, and I find that when Moses ascended the mountain, the children of Israel rebelled, and made a golden calf and worshiped it, and it brought a curse upon them. This bank will be a greater curse."

President Jackson was trying to force the Second Bank of the United States to turn over its books on the accounting of pensions of the veterans of the Revolutionary War, but the Bank refused, much like Ben Bernanke and his predecessors have done in recent times when faced with requests for an audit of the Federal Reserve. The cashier of the Second Bank stated firmly that the Bank is a corporation and, like a citizen of the United States, has a right to certain rights, privileges and duties. One of those is the right to privacy.

Jackson further added: "I have no hostility to the bank; I am willing it should expire in peace; but if it does persist in its war with the government, I have a measure in contemplation which will destroy it at once, and which I am resolved to apply, be the consequences to individuals what they may."

President Jackson's veto message was written by George Bancroft in 1834:

"The United States Bank, as at present constituted, ought never to be renewed. The reasons are obvious.

"The capital is too vast. In proportion to the wealth of the country, it is the largest moneyed monopoly in the world. . . . Republican America, the Virgin of the New World, the Government which is especially charged by wholesome legislation to prevent all extreme inequalities of fortune, has surpassed every country in Europe in the lavish concession of influence and privileges to a moneyed corporation.

"Political influence is steadily tending to the summit level of property.

"When a life and trust company ask for privileges, which enable capital to consume the moderate profits of the farmer by tempting him to incur the hazards of debt, it is the clamor of capital, deafening the voice of benevolence and legislative wisdom.

"When the creditor demands that the debtor may once more be allowed to pledge his body and his personal freedom, it is the clamor of capital.

"When 'vested rights' claim a veto on legislation, and assert themselves as the law paramount in defiance of the constitution which makes the common good the supreme rule, it is the clamor of capital, desiring to renew one of the abuses of feudal institutions.

"When the usurer invokes the aid of society to enforce the contracts, which he has wrung without mercy from the feverish hopes of pressing necessity, it is the clamor of capital, which like the grave never says, It is enough.

"When employers combine to reduce the wages of labor, and at the same time threaten an indictment for conspiracy against the combinations of workmen, it is the clamor of capital

"The feud between the capitalist and the laborer, the house of Have and the house of Want, is as old as social union, and can never be entirely quieted; but he who will act with moderation, prefer facts to theories, and remember that every thing in this world is relative and not absolute, will see that the violence of the contest may be stilled, if the unreasonable demands of personal interests are subjected to the decisions of even-handed justice. . . ."

In an editorial in the *Boston Daily Advertiser and Patriot*, in 1832, the paper made a curious admission:

"The national bank [Second Bank of the United States], though not properly a political institution, is one of the most important and valuable instruments that are used in the practical administration of the government."

Though not properly a political institution. . . .

This was one of the earliest statements showing that these central banks that were installed in the US by the Jesuits and House of Rothschild were *private* banks . . . *private* corporations.

Not surprisingly, two assassination attempts were made on President Jackson's life. The second was considered a miracle, when the Jesuit-installed assassin, Richard Lawrence, fired twice from his derringers, each of which misfired in the moist air of January 30, 1835.

"Old Hickory" was saved by the uncharacteristically damp winter of Washington, DC.

Seems that the Jesuits and the House of Rothschild didn't understand what we US Army Rangers know all too well: keep your powder *dry*.

"Old Hickory" is still the only US president to pay down the national debt, which so infuriated the Jesuits and the House of Rothschild that they once again tanned the backside of America by causing the panic of 1837, followed by a five-year depression, the worst in US history to that point.

The Jesuits assassinated at least six US presidents. The murder of Abraham Lincoln will be discussed in an upcoming book that was originally published in 1922, *The Suppressed Truth About the Assassination of Abraham Lincoln*, under the title *How the Jesuits Murdered President Abraham Lincoln*, and thus will not be explored here.

In a bold move, the Jesuits murdered another US president and all the members of his family, save one son who was allowed to live as a messenger of what may become of those who oppose the policies of the evil Jesuits.

The United States Federal Reserve Act of 1913

President Woodrow Wilson was directed by the Jesuits to allow the House of Rothschild to take full control over his office and permit their agent Paul Warburg to establish formal laws that enacted the US Federal Reserve Bank and the federal income tax.

In his book, *The New Freedom: A Call For the Emancipation of the Generous Energies of a People*, Wilson lamented over his ill-conceived decision to support Warburg in establishing the Federal Reserve Bank of the United States:

"This money trust, or, as it should be more properly called, this credit trust, of which Congress has begun an investigation, is no myth; it is no imaginary thing. It is not an ordinary trust like another. It doesn't do business every day. It does business only when there is occasion to do business. You can sometimes do something large when it isn't watching, but when it is watching, you can't do much. And I have seen men squeezed by it; I have seen men who, as they themselves expressed it, were put 'out of business by Wall Street,' because Wall Street found them inconvenient and didn't want their competition."

Wilson further elaborated on the fears over the powerful Jesuits and its Stepford offspring, the House of Rothschild:

"Since I entered politics, I have chiefly had men's views confided to me privately. Some of the biggest men in the United States, in the field of commerce and manufacture, are afraid of somebody, are afraid of something. They know that there is a power somewhere so organized, so subtle, so watchful, so interlocked, so complete, so pervasive, that they had better not speak above their breath when they speak in condemnation of it."

Shortly after passage of the new Federal Reserve bill, on December 23, 1913, Congressman Charles A. Lindbergh stated:

"This Act established the most gigantic trust on earth. When the President signs this bill, the invisible government by the Monetary Power will be legalized. The People may not know it immediately but the day of reckoning is only a few years away."

Years later, on June 10, 1932, a man considered by many as the expert on all things the Fed, Congressman Louis T. McFadden, Chairman of the House Committee on Banking and Currency, addressed the US House of Representatives:

"Mr. Chairman, we have in this country one of the most corrupt institutions the world has ever known. I refer to the Federal Reserve Board and the Federal Reserve Banks. The Federal Reserve Board has cheated the Government of the United States and the people of the United States out of enough money to pay the national debt.

"The depredations and iniquities of the Federal Reserve Board and the Federal Reserve Banks acting together have cost this country enough money to pay the national debt several times over. This evil institution has impoverished and ruined the People of the United States; has bankrupted itself; and has practically bankrupted our government. It has done this through the defects of the law under which it operates, through the maladministration of that law by the Federal Reserve Board, and through the corrupt practices of the moneyed vultures who control it."

Like hundreds of other politicians who opposed the Jesuits, the good Congressman McFadden was murdered after two attempts for his continual battle against them. He was the last Congressman to genuinely oppose The First Sphere of Influence.

Please do not be fooled by men like former Congressman Ron Paul. He was "controlled political opposition," someone who purports to be on the side of We The People but is actually a member of one of the Jesuits' political parties. Congressman Paul "complained" about how the Federal Reserve refused to allow an audit of its books and for its lack of transparency, and did it from a position of power and safety for 25 years. And "failed" at every turn.

If Paul truly had been the opposition, like our beloved Congressman McFadden, the Jesuits would've murdered him long ago. Men like Paul are out there in increasing numbers, all seemingly opposing the Jesuits and the House of Rothschild in the media, but in reality they're just there to control the population of people who oppose the actions of the Jesuits, and to give We The People an official "voice." Unfortunately, it is a false voice, one whose notes are never echoed in the deep, dark chambers where the Jesuits lurk and plot.

The Great Depression (1929~1941)

This period in US and world history provides an excellent example of how the Jesuits and the House of Rothschild first expand a nation's money supply by printing billions of dollars and dumping it into an economy, then after a period of time call in all loans and credits, thus collapsing the entire economy.

Starting on 29 October 1929, also known as Black Tuesday, We The People lost our businesses, business property, jobs, homes, land, life savings, and much more . . . faith in our own government to protect us from the ravages of the the Jesuits and the House of Rothschild.

The result: a great depression that lasted more than 10 years.

You'll recall from Chapter 3 these same machinations occurred during the sack of the Weimar Republic only a decade before.

Who Really Owns Your Gold, America?

I could go on and on for another thousand pages, listing the various global wars and conflicts, country and government takeovers, depressions, recessions, assassinations, murders, and other intrigues, some directly instigated, but most exacerbated, by the the Jesuits and the House of Rothschild. This dark cabal is well familiar with the cycles of celestial, solar and lunar events, all of which mediate and modulate life and geophysical events on earth. Worst of all, this cabal chooses to amplify the negative influences of these cycles for their own gain.

And to the detriment of We The People.

Your gold is not owned by you. Never has.

It is owned, and usually held in "trust," by the Jesuits and the House of Rothschild. Unless you actually possess physical gold, you don't own anything. Only a slip of paper, a certificate, that states you "own" gold that is not in your physical possession. And if you do actually hold your own gold, it can be confiscated at any time by the Jesuits, as it was between 1933 and 1974. They need not give you advance notice before they break down your door, search your home and collect what they claim is theirs.

Again, recall the confiscation of gold from 1933 to 1974. No ordinary citizen was immune.

Your owning your gold is only an illusion, Dear Reader.

You own nothing.

Not even your own home or land. As stated previously, allodial property in America or anywhere does not exist. It is all the property of a dark cabal of men who loathe you and wish to drive you to bankruptcy.

Or suicide.

Take your pick.

They're happy with either one, but they would prefer you dead. . . .

Those Americans in denial about the information I have presented here should take great care when raising a head from the safety of that big hole in the sand . . . they may be decapitated by the facts.

Some Final Thoughts. . . .

Our best revenge, if we must have it, is to educate everyone worldwide about the human controllers of Mother Earth, The Society of Jesus, the Jesuits, and their accountants, the House of Rothschild, their checkered history, methods of conducting all levels of business in politics and economics, their strengths and weaknesses and, perhaps most important of all, how to counter their every move in this deadly game of global chess. Beyond this, our truly best revenge is personal success.

If all else fails, take comfort knowing that everything in the Universe runs in cycles and that what goes around, comes around . . . *eventually.*"

Postscript

About The Author

For more than 30 years, William Dean A. Garner has done anecdotal, and for the past seven years intensive, research on the human element that controls our planet: the Jesuits and the House of Rothschild. He writes and speaks about the dangers of this global cartel that is slowly destroying our very fabric of peace, freedom and liberty. In 2015, he handed over his papers, books and research to Sean Maclaren, who was commissioned to write the two sequels to *Who Really Owns Your Gold*. The first, *Arcanum*, was published in May 2015. The second, *Romanic Depression*, will be published in late 2015.

A Note On The Bibliography

Over 30 years, William Garner has read more than 1,000 books, newspaper and magazine articles, and other primary-source materials, plus interviewed hundreds of insiders, whistleblowers and ordinary citizens on the subject of the Jesuits. To support his current book, he chose to use less than 10% of that valuable and powerful arsenal, just over 100 references. A more comprehensive list (more than 200 books) can be found in Sean Maclaren's *Arcanum: A critical analysis of the original 36 sermons of Jmmanuel, the man known to the world as Jesus Christ.*

When connecting the dots, Garner discovered some interesting patterns, not the least of which was that certain classes of books (e.g. Astrology, Celestiophysics) fell off the radar in the late 1800s. This corresponded to the time when the Jesuits had purchased a great many of the book and newspaper and magazine publishing companies throughout the world. It is no coincidence that the Jesuits suppressed much of the information he has been able to reveal in his current book.

By the grace of a few brave whistleblowers and malcontents who had previously worked for the Jesuits, we now have an accurate, but by no means full, accounting of the evil deeds done by the Jesuits and their minions. Surprisingly, too, it does not take too many dots to show definitively a design, a pattern, a few blurry faces, or a single important entity among many.

In support of this current book, you will find many important and precious primary-source references from the 1800s, with very few from the 1900s and only a handful from the 2000s. What does this pattern of suppression of valuable materials suggest to you? Dear Reader, please indulge your senses, see for yourself what is real . . . and what is fiction, neatly dressed up by the Jesuits as "fact."

Canada-US Civil Assistance Plan (CAP)

The following 10-page unclassified document outlines in relative detail the plans for Canadian and US forces to cross the northern border of the US and "assist" each other's civilian and/or militaries during "civil support operations: floods, forest fires, hurricanes, earthquakes, and effects of a terrorist attack." The US also has plans for other members of the United Nations to cross our borders in the event of a civil uprising.

Signed on February 14, 2008 in San Antonio, Texas, the CAP circumvents the US Posse Comitatus Act of 1878, which forbids the use of a military force in the capacity of law enforcement on non-federal property, i.e. state, county and local lands. For more than 65 years, the Jesuits have attempted to circumvent this important Act, which effectively protects US citizens from attacks by their own military forces, especially during periods of civil unrest.

The term civil unrest, which our own government interprets very liberally, can apply to peaceful sit-ins on college campuses, and peaceful and respectful protest marches like those on Wall Street in September 2011, when New York City Police used tear gas and aggressive force to subdue and arrest peaceful protesters, most of them female, armed only with protest signs and placards. Also witness the Jesuit-designed Occupy America sleepovers, in which We The People were beaten, tear-gassed, terrorized and arrested by American law-enforcement officers in dozens of cities across the US. Worse, the Jesuits implanted dozens of law-enforcement officers into civilian crowds to incite fights and riots, thus providing an excuse for these very law-enforcement agencies to act in even more brutal ways.

The tragedy of CAP is not in its wording but in the spirit in which it was meant: to subdue We The People into submission when they voice dissent against their oppressive government. CAP effectively signals one of the hallmarks of a fascist regime: silent and deadly oppression of the voice and action of We The People. And they carry out their actions not unlike virus or bacteria: first they secretly invade you . . . then they slowly and purposefully consume you from within, leaving only an empty, malleable and obedient shell.

UNCLASSIFIED/~~FOR OFFICIAL USE ONLY~~

CANADA COMMAND

AND

UNITED STATES NORTHERN COMMAND

14 February 2008

CANADA – US CIVIL ASSISTANCE PLAN (CAP)

CANUS CAP-08

UNCLASSIFIED/~~FOR OFFICIAL USE ONLY~~

Canada Command   HQ US Northern Command
MGen George R. Pearkes Bldg   250 Vandenberg St
101 Colonel By Drive   Peterson Air Force Base
Ottawa, Ontario, CA K1A 0K2   Colorado, USA 80914
                                               14 February 2008

CANADA - US CIVIL ASSISTANCE PLAN (CAP)
BASE PLAN

References: See Annex W [Note: Annexes are exempt from mandatory disclosure and are being withheld because these records are pre-decisional plans. See 5 USC 552(b)(5)]

1. Situation

    a. General. The purpose of the Canada-United States Civil Assistance
Plan (CAP) is to provide a framework for the military of one nation to provide
support to the military of the other nation in the performance of civil support
operations (e.g., floods, forest fires, hurricanes, earthquakes, and effects of a
terrorist attack).

        (1) Support covered under this plan will only be provided when
agreed to by appropriate authorities in both the Government of Canada and the
United States Government.

        (2) When approved, military forces from one nation augment the
other nation's forces in civil support operations. Support under this plan is not
provided directly to civil authorities, but rather to the other nation's military.

        (3) Support for law enforcement operations is not covered in this
plan and will be included in the Canada – United States Combined Defense
Plan (CDP).

        (4) Guidance and direction to develop this plan is derived from the
Canada – United States Basic Defense Document (BDD), 08 July 2006 (Ref 1f).
This plan may be used alone, or concurrent with the Canada-US Combined
Defense Plan or other national plans. The Commander, Canada Command
(Comd Canada COM) and Commander, US Northern Command
(CDRUSNORTHCOM) are the designated planning agents for the development
of this plan.

    b. Federal Coordination of Emergency Response. The Canadian
Department of Foreign Affairs and International Trade (DFAIT), acting on behalf
of the Government of Canada (GoC), and the US Department of State (DOS),
acting on behalf of the United States Government (USG), will, upon receipt of a
formal request for, or offer of mutual assistance, coordinate an agreed upon
bilateral response that may include military support.

UNCLASSIFIED/~~FOR OFFICIAL USE ONLY~~

(1) In the United States, coordination of foreign assistance for a disaster in the United States is conducted per the International Assistance System Concept of Operations.

c. Area of Responsibility (AOR). AOR is defined as the common areas of responsibility for Primary Agencies (Public Safety Canada (PS) and Department Of Homeland Security (DHS)), and the Canada -US (CANUS) Region (i.e., Canada and the Continental United States (CONUS), Alaska, US Virgin Islands, and Puerto Rico, including each nation's territorial seas).

d. Opposing Force. Opposing forces are not expected during the conduct of operations described in this plan. However, when planning and conducting operations where the military forces of one nation are supporting the military forces of the other nation that are conducting civil support operations, commanders should consider the following Anti-Terrorism/Force Protection issues: (1) Terrorists organizations could conduct operations against the Canadian or US force, or in the civil support operations area; (2) State/provincial and local police capabilities could be severely degraded in the area of operations, allowing a corresponding rise in criminal activity that could affect the Canadian or US force; and (3) Environmental factors ranging from weather to contamination and disease could significantly affect the Canadian or US forces.

e. Friendly

(1) CANADA

(a) The Department of Foreign Affairs and International Trade (DFAIT). DFAIT is responsible on behalf of the GoC for facilitating requests for international military assistance.

(b) Public Safety Canada (PS). The Minister of Public Safety is assigned primary responsibility within the GoC to coordinate the federal response in crisis and consequence management situations within Canada.

(c) Department of National Defence (DND) / Canadian Forces (CF). The CF may, upon request, provide support to PS, other federal departments and agencies, provincial/territorial and municipal authorities pursuant to the National Defence Act (NDA), or other legal authority. Comd Canada COM is the responsible CF operational commander within the Canada COM AOR defined as Canada, the continental United States, Mexico, and the maritime approaches to North America.

(2) UNITED STATES

2

UNCLASSIFIED/~~FOR OFFICIAL USE ONLY~~

UNCLASSIFIED/~~FOR OFFICIAL USE ONLY~~

(a) Department of State (DOS). The Department of State is responsible for coordinating with other nations for disaster assistance, including military assistance. (Ref 3l).

(b) Department of Homeland Security (DHS). The Secretary of DHS is the principal federal official (PFO) for US domestic incident management.

(c) Department of Defense (DOD). In accordance with the National Response Plan (Ref 3k) DOD may, upon request, provide support to DHS and other federal agencies for domestic Defense Support of Civil Authorities (DSCA). Upon Secretary of Defense approval, CDRUSNORTHCOM is the supported combatant commander with responsibility to coordinate defense support to federal agencies within that portion of the United States within CDRUSNORTHCOM's AOR.

f. Assumptions

(1) Requirements for military support of civilian authorities could be fulfilled by either nation's military. However, the nation providing cross-border military support will not fulfill these requirements directly to the other nation's civilian authorities, but rather to the other nation's military.

(2) Operations will typically occur in a permissive environment.

g. Legal Considerations. The United States and Canada are Parties to the North Atlantic Treaty Organization (NATO) Status of Forces Agreement (SOFA), dated August 23, 1953.

(1) Military Emergency Response

(a). Canadian Forces (CF). In Canada, as per Canada Command Direction for Domestic Operations (Ref 2i), local commanders are expected to respond promptly to a request for assistance, within their approval authority, by providing an immediate CF response to an emergency to save lives, prevent human suffering, or mitigate property damage. However, for foreign disaster assistance, the GoC must approve the request.

(b). US Armed Forces. In emergency situations the SecDef can provide foreign disaster assistance in order to save human lives, where there is not sufficient time to seek the prior initial concurrence of the Secretary of State. The SecDef shall advise, and seek the concurrence of the Secretary of State as soon as practicable thereafter (Ref 3b).

3

UNCLASSIFIED/~~FOR OFFICIAL USE ONLY~~

UNCLASSIFIED/~~FOR OFFICIAL USE ONLY~~

(2) <u>US Foreign Consequence Management versus US Foreign Disaster Assistance</u>

(a) Only the President may order US military forces to execute foreign consequence management missions. DOS is the lead agency (Ref 4f).

(b) When directed by the President or by the Secretary of Defense, with the concurrence of the Secretary of State, DOD provides foreign disaster assistance support in coordination with DOS. DOS is the lead agency (Ref 3b and 4g).

(3) <u>Use of Force</u>

(a) <u>CF Rules of Engagement (ROE)</u>. If ROE are required for CF personnel deployed in the United States to support the US forces engaged in Defense Support of Civil Authorities, the ROE will be requested by the Canadian commander and authorized in accordance with B-GG-005-004/AF-005 dated 2001-06-01 Use of Force in CF Operations (Revision 1).

(b) <u>Standing Rules of Engagement (SROE) for DOD forces</u>. Implementation guidance on the application of force for mission accomplishment and the exercise of self-defense is contained in (Ref 4d). DOD forces will be trained on SROE before employment.

(4) <u>Right of Self Defense</u>

(a) <u>Canadian Forces</u>. Both international law and Canadian domestic laws recognize the authority to use appropriate force in self-defense, up to and including deadly force. Without further written or oral direction, CF personnel are entitled to use force in self-defense to protect oneself; other members of the Canadian Forces; and non-Canadian military personnel who are attached or seconded to a Canadian force against a hostile act or hostile intent (Ref 2c).

(b) <u>US Forces</u>. US unit commanders always retain the inherent right and obligation to exercise unit self-defense in response to a hostile act or demonstrated hostile intent (Ref 4d).

(5) There are no standing CANUS rules of engagement or rules for the use of force. Consequently, every mission will require unique guidance to deployed forces. Forces from one nation deployed to support the forces of the other nation will comply with authorized ROE and right of self-defense consistent with the laws of the supported nation. The ROE and right of self-defense will be designated in respective national operation / execute orders.

4

UNCLASSIFIED/~~FOR OFFICIAL USE ONLY~~

UNCLASSIFIED/~~FOR OFFICIAL USE ONLY~~

2. Mission. When directed by the Government of Canada and the US President or Secretary of Defense, the commander(s) of designated Canadian and US military forces will provide support to the other nation's military force that are engaged in civil support operations in order to save lives, prevent human suffering and mitigate damage to property.

3. Execution

  a. Concept of Operations

    (1) Commanders' Intent. A timely response to a federal request for military assistance in a national or cross-border civil emergency will be critical to save lives, prevent human suffering and mitigate damage to property. The role of the military in civil emergencies is to provide support to Primary Agencies and first responders. As such, it is essential that Canadian and US military forces work closely in support of federal authorities to coordinate national and bilateral civil support when requested and authorized. As the nature of every emergency situation will be unique, Canadian and US military forces must maintain a flexible, adaptive approach that supports rapid decision-making and a collaborative response to requests for bilateral support. The key to success will be the mechanisms used to coordinate this support in an emergency. Thus, the establishment, maintenance, and regular exercise of bilateral coordination mechanisms are the principal requirements of this plan.

    (2) Concept for the Military Forces of one Nation to Support the Military Forces of the other that are engaged in Civil Support Operations. Close coordination and synchronization with the respective lead federal agencies responsible for national and international crisis and consequence response is essential to the provision of effective support. DHS is principally responsible for the coordination of a response to a US domestic incident. PS is assigned primary responsibility to coordinate the federal response in crisis and consequence management situations within Canada. Responsibility for the detailed coordination of a Canadian response to a US incident will depend upon the nature, severity and location of the incident; DFAIT and PS are the designated coordination agencies with the lead among departments determined on a case-specific basis. The Department of State (DOS) and DHS will normally coordinate the provision of a US response to a Canadian incident. DFAIT and DOS provide the formal diplomatic mechanism for requests, offers and acceptance of bilateral assistance on behalf of their respective Governments.

    (3) In concert with and in support of these diplomatic efforts, the CF, represented by Comd Canada COM, and the US Armed Forces, represented by CDRUSNORTHCOM, will develop potential options for the military forces of one nation to support the military forces of the other nation that are engaged in

5

UNCLASSIFIED/~~FOR OFFICIAL USE ONLY~~

UNCLASSIFIED/~~FOR OFFICIAL USE ONLY~~

civil support operations, subject to direction received from the Chief of the Defence Staff (CDS) and Chairman of the Joint Chiefs of Staff (CJCS) and/or SecDef respectively. In Canada, Comd Canada COM will present military options to the CDS, who will subsequently present options and seek the approval of the Government of Canada to deploy military forces to the United States. In the United States, CDRUSNORTHCOM will present military options to the SecDef who will subsequently seek the approval of the President to deploy military forces to Canada.

(4) Civil Support operations described in this plan will be conducted in accordance with the host nation's civil support plan(s).

b. End State

(1) A cooperative and well-coordinated timely response to national requests for military assistance in relation to natural disasters or other major emergencies in Canada or the United States.

(2) Forces have completed all assigned missions and redeployment is complete.

c. Tasks to Commanders Supporting the CAP

(1) Commander, Canada Command (Comd Canada COM)

(a) Maintain situational awareness and information sharing with CDRUSNORTHCOM.

(b) Coordinate planning for the possible employment of US forces in support of Canada Command's support of civil authorities in Canada.

(c) On order, coordinate the provision of CF assistance to designated US Armed Forces conducting DSCA in the United States.

(d) On order, task subordinate commanders to support US forces engaged in USNORTHCOM DSCA operations in the United States.

(e) Maintain national procedures to coordinate requests for US military forces and integrate those forces into Canada COM operations in support of civil authorities in Canada.

(f) Conduct a review of this plan as required or at a minimum every two years.

UNCLASSIFIED/~~FOR OFFICIAL USE ONLY~~

UNCLASSIFIED/~~FOR OFFICIAL USE ONLY~~

(g) Plan and conduct combined exercises in support of this plan.

(2) Commander, US Northern Command (CDRUSNORTHCOM)

(a) Maintain situational awareness and information sharing with the Commander, Canada COM.

(b) Coordinate planning for the possible employment of Canadian forces in support of USNORTHCOM's support of primary civil agencies in the United States.

(c) On order, coordinate the provision of US Armed Forces assistance to designated Canadian forces conducting support of civil authorities in Canada.

(d) When directed by the SecDef, task supporting commanders to provide forces and resources to support Canadian forces engaged in civil support operations.

(e) Request forces and resources via a Request for Forces to the US Joint Staff.

(f) Maintain national military procedures to coordinate requests for and integrate Canadian forces in DSCA operations in the United States.

(g) Conduct a review of this plan as required or at a minimum every two years.

(h) Plan and conduct combined exercises in support of this plan.

d. Coordinating Instructions

(1) Implementation. This plan is effective for planning upon receipt.

(2) Liaison and Planning. Direct liaison is authorized (DIRLAUTH) between the militaries of both nations for planning, information sharing and situational awareness. The state Governors and provincial authorities in the Pacific Northwest, Prairie and Northeastern regions have established mutual aid compacts for cross border emergency support to save lives, prevent human suffering, and reduce great property damage. Every effort should be made to maintain situational awareness of these existing bilateral civilian regional

7

UNCLASSIFIED/~~FOR OFFICIAL USE ONLY~~

UNCLASSIFIED/~~FOR OFFICIAL USE ONLY~~

planning groups to ensure support to the other nation's forces is effective and efficient.

(3) Execution Authority. Execution authority rests with Commanders Canada COM and USNORTHCOM.

(4) Situational Awareness. Both nations will take advantage of existing communications infrastructure to maintain situational awareness required to plan for bilateral support. Both nations will share information to the maximum extent allowed by national laws, agreements, and policy.

(5) Training. In accordance with international agreements and implementing procedures, cross-border movement of military resources is authorized for training and exercises in preparation for bilateral military-to – military civil support. Activities in support of civil authorities beyond the scope of this plan will require mission specific training to be conducted prior to employment.

4. Administration and Logistics

a. Concept of Support. Each nation will be responsible for providing support to its own forces. However, where and when it is feasible, every effort should be made to use existing mutual support agreements, memoranda of understanding, and implementing arrangements to support and sustain Canadian and US military forces. Military planners will submit their transportation requirements through respective national channels for determination of which agreements/programs will be used to provide the necessary support.

5. Command and Control

a. Command

(1) Command Relationships. Bilateral support described in this plan will occur under existing structures and command authorities. Command relationships for supporting forces will be defined based on the circumstances of the operation and delineated in respective national operation and execution orders.

(a) Canada. Comd Canada COM exercises operational command (OPCOM) of CF forces assigned by the CDS for the purposes of coordinating assistance to civil authorities. Regional Joint Task Force Commanders (RJTF Comds) exercise OPCON of forces assigned by Comd Canada COM for the execution of an operation. In Canada, OPCOM is the authority granted to a commander to assign missions or tasks to subordinate

8

UNCLASSIFIED/~~FOR OFFICIAL USE ONLY~~

UNCLASSIFIED/~~FOR OFFICIAL USE ONLY~~

commanders, to deploy units, to reassign forces, and to retain or delegate operational/tactical command or control as may be deemed necessary. OPCON is the authority delegated to a commander to direct forces assigned so that the commander may accomplish specific missions or tasks that are usually limited by function, time, or location; to deploy units concerned and to retain or assign tactical control of those units. If the requirement develops for separate employment, the higher commander must approve the change. (Ref 2y).

(b) United States. CDRUSNORTHCOM exercises operational control (OPCON) of all allocated US forces (less CDRUSTRANSCOM). In the United States, OPCON is command authority that may be exercised by commanders at any echelon at or below the level of combatant command. OPCON is inherent in combatant command (command authority) and may be delegated within the command. (Ref 4jj).

b. Command, Control, Communication and Computer (C4) Systems. As directed by the BDD, Canada COM and USNORTHCOM will ensure network-enabled capabilities to enhance information sharing, collaborative planning and rapid decision making to support bilateral operations described in this plan.

M. J. DUMAIS
Lieutenant-General, CF
Commander,
Canada Command

VICTOR E. RENUART
General, USAF
Commander,
US Northern Command

9

Bibliography

Adams, Brooks. 1896. *The Gold Standard: An Historical Study*. Robert Beall, Bookseller. Washington, DC.

Aldred, Cyril. 1961. *The Egyptians*. Frederick A. Praeger, New York, NY.

Astle, David. 1975. *The Babylonian Woe: A Study of the Origin of Certain Banking Practices, and Their Effect on the Events of Ancient History, Written in the Light of the Present Day*. Published as a private edition. Toronto, ON.

Balla, Ignatius. 1913. *The Romance of the Rothschilds*. Eveleigh Nash. London, England.

Beard AG, Williams PJS, Mitchell NJ and Muller HG. 2001. "A special climatology of planetary waves and tidal variability." *Journal of Atmospheric and Solar-Terrestrial Physics*, 63:9, pp. 801-811.

Berman, Eric. 2010. Personal interviews conducted by William Dean A. Garner.

Bernstein, Peter L. 2000. *The Power of Gold: The History of an Obsession*. John Wiley and Sons. New York, NY.

Bungener, L.F. 1855. *History of the Council of Trent*. Harper and Brothers, Publishers. New York, NY.

Bill of Rights of the United States. December 15, 1791. United States National Archives. www.archives.gov/exhibits/charters/bill_of_rights_transcript.html. Accessed and vetted 12 April 2010, 08 December 2011.

Brands, HW. 2002. *The Age of Gold: The California Gold Rush and the New American Dream*. Doubleday. New York, NY.

Brzezinski, Zbigniew. 1983. *Power and Principle: Memoirs of the National Security Advisor, 1977-1981*. Farrar, Straus, Giroux. New York, NY.

Brzezinski, Zbigniew. 1997. *The Grand Chessboard: American Primacy and Its Geostrategic Imperatives*. Basic Books. New York, NY.

Brzezinski, Zbigniew and Scowcroft, Brent. 2008. *America and the World: Conversations on the Future of American Foreign Policy*. Basic Books. New York, NY.

Butler, Smedley D. 1935. *War is a Racket*. Round Table Press. New York, NY.

Carlson, John Roy. 1943. *Under Cover: My Four Years in the Nazi Underworld of America: The Amazing Revelation of How Axis Agents and Our Enemies Within Are Now Plotting to Destroy the United States*. E.P. Dutton and Company. New York, NY.

Chevalier, Michel. 1859. *On the Probable Fall in the Value of Gold: The Commercial and Social Consequences Which May Ensue, and the Measures Which It Invites*. D. Appleton and Company. New York, NY.

Chiniquy, Charles. 1886. *Fifty Years in the Church of Rome*. Fleming H. Revell Company. New York, NY.

"Conduct of the Administration." 1832. In Chapter VIII, "The Bank." *The Boston Daily Advertiser and Patriot*, Boston, MA.

Constitution of the United States. 1787. United States National Archives. www.archives.gov/exhibits/charters/constitution_transcript.html. Accessed and vetted 12 April 2010, 08 December 2011.

Corti, Count Egon Caesar. 1928. *The Rise of the House of Rothschild: 1770-1830*. Cosmopolitan Book Corporation. New York, NY.

Corti, Count Egon Caesar. 1928. *The Reign of the House of Rothschild: 1830-1871*. Cosmopolitan Book Corporation. New York, NY.

Creighton, Christopher. 1996. *Operation James Bond: The Last Great Secret of the Second World War*. Simon and Schuster. London, England.

Crozier, Alfred Owen. 1912. *U.S. Money vs. Corporation Currency: "Aldrich Plan." Wall Street Confessions!* The Magnet Company. Cincinnati, OH

Daniel, T. Cushing. 1911. *Daniel On Real Money*. The Monetary Educational Bureau. Washington, DC.

Daniel, T. Cushing. 1912. *High Cost of Living, Cause-Remedy*. The Monetary Educational Bureau. Washington, DC.

Daniel, T. Cushing. 1916. *The Betrayal of the People*. The Monetary Educational Bureau. Washington, DC.

Daniel, T. Cushing. 1917. *The Real Issue, Democracy Against Plutocracy*. The Monetary Educational Bureau. Washington, DC.

Daniel, T. Cushing. 1919. *No Plutocratic Peace But a Democratic Victory*. The Monetary Educational Bureau. Washington, DC.

Daniel, T. Cushing. 1924. *Real Money Versus False Money—Bank Credits*. The Monetary Educational Bureau. Washington, DC.

Declaration of Independence of the United States. 04 July 1776. United States National Archives. www.archives.gov/exhibits/charters/declaration_ transcript.html. Accessed and vetted 12 April 2010, 08 December 2011.

Dewey, Edward R. and Dakin, Edwin F. 1947. *Cycles: The Science of Prediction*. Henry Holt and Company. New York, NY.

Eden, Dan. 04 December 2009. "Fake Gold Bars In Ft. Knox." mondovista. com/fakegoldx.html. Accessed and vetted 12 April 2010, 08 December 2011.

Eizenstat, Stuart. 04 December 1997. "Closing Plenary Statement at the London Conference on Nazi Gold." www.state.gov/www/policy_ remarks/971204_eizen_nazigold.html. Accessed and vetted 13 April 2010, 08 December 2011.

Eksteins, Modris. 1975. *Limits of Reason: The German Democratic Press and the Collapse of Weimar Democracy*. Oxford University Press. London, England.

Elon, Amos. 1996. Founder: *A Portrait of the First Rothschild and His Time*. Viking. New York, NY.

Evans, T. Rhys. 1888. *The Council of Trent: A Study of Romish Tactics*. The Religious Tract Society. London, England.

Farrell, Joseph P. *Babylon's Banksters: The Alchemy of Deep Physics, High Finance and Ancient Religion.* Feral House, Port Townsend, WA.

Fergusson, Adam. 1975. *When Money Dies: The Nightmare of the Weimar Collapse.* William Kimber, Ltd. London, England.

Ganz, David L. "Gold All There When Ft. Knox Opened Doors." www.numismaster.com/ta/numis/Article.jsp?ad=article&ArticleId=7634#. Accessed and vetted 26 November 2009, 26 November 2011.

Garner, William Dean A. Direct personal observations of The First Sphere of Influence in more than 100 countries across the globe, especially between the years 1980-2015.

Garner, William Dean A. 2010. Personal letter to Dr. Zbigniew Brzezinski.

Gold Standard Defence Association. 1895. *The Gold Standard, 1895.* Nos. 1 to 12. Cassell and Company, Ltd. London, England.

Gray, Michael. 11 April 2010. "Metal$ are in the pits: Trader blows whistle on gold & silver price manipulation." *New York Post.* New York, NY.

Haberler, Gottfried. 1946. *Prosperity and Depression: A Theoretical Analysis of Cyclical Movements.* United Nations. Lake Success, NY.

"Historical Gold Prices: 1833-2008." www.nma.org/pdf/gold/his_gold_prices.pdf. Accessed and vetted 12 April 2010, 08 December 2011.

"How The Rothschild Fortune of $2,000,000,000 Was Made." 26 January 1913. *New York Times.* New York, NY.

Iden, V. Gilmore. 1914. *The Federal Reserve Act of 1913: History and Digest.* The National Bank News. Philadelphia, PA.

Jefferson, Thomas. 1903. *The Writings of Thomas Jefferson*, 20 volumes, Vol. 10. Published by the order of the Joint Committee of Congress, issued under the auspices of the Thomas Jefferson Memorial Association. Andrew A. Lipscomb, Editor-in-Chief, and Albert Ellery Bergh, Managing Editor. Washington, DC.

Jevons, William Stanley. 1863. *A Serious Fall in the Value of Gold Ascertained, and Its Social Effects Set Forth.* Edward Stanford. London, England.

Jevons, William Stanley. 1879. "Sun-Spots and Commercial Crises." *Nature,* Volume 19:495, pp. 588-590. London, England.

Jevons, William Stanley. 1882. "The Solar-Commercial Cycle." *Nature,* Volume 19:495, pp. 588-590. London, England.

Jevons, William Stanley. 1884. *Investigations in Currency and Finance.* Macmillan and Company. London, England.

Joseph, Chief Young. April 1879. "An Indian's Views of Indians Affairs." *North American Review,* 128. Cedar Falls, IA.

Kemp, John. 1878. "Commercial Crises and Sun-Spots." *Nature,* Volume 19:475, pp. 97-98. London, England.

Kennedy, David M. and Cohen, Bailey. 2006. *The American Pageant,* 13th ed. Houghton Mifflin Company. Boston, MA.

Lease, Mary. 12 August 1896, Cooper Union Hall, New York, NY. spartacus-educational.com/USAleaseM.htm. Accessed 20 June 2015.

Lehmann, L.H. 1944. *Behind the Dictators: A Factual Analysis of the Relationship of Nazi-Fascism and Roman Catholicism. Second enlarged edition.* Agora Publishing Company. New York, NY.

Lewis, Nathan. 2007. *Gold: The Once and Future Money.* John Wiley and Sons. New York, NY.

Lindbergh, Charles A. 1913. *Banking and Currency and the Money Trust.* National Capital Press, Inc. Washington, DC.

Livingston, James. 1986. *Origins of the Federal Reserve System: Money, Class and Corporate Capitalism, 1890–1913.* Cornell University Press. Ithaca, NY

"London Gold Market: 1660-2004." www.goldfixing.com/goldfixing.pdf. Accessed and vetted 10 April 2010, 08 December 2011.

McCarty, Burke. 1922. *The Suppressed Truth About the Assassination of Abraham Lincoln.* Washington, DC.

Makow, Henry. 2009. *Illuminati: The Cult That Hijacked the World.* Silas Green. Winnipeg, Canada.

Mayer, Milton. 1955. *They Thought They Were Free: The Germans 1933-45.* The University of Chicago Press. Chicago, IL.

Marshall, James W. 1857. In "The Discovery of Gold In California." *Hutchings' California Magazine.* Hutchings and Rosenfield. San Francisco, CA.

Mendham, Joseph. 1834. *Memoirs of the Council of Trent.* James Duncan. London, England.

Mitchell, Paul Andrew. "31 Questions and Answers About the Internal Revenue Service", rev. 3.7, Seattle, WA. www.supremelaw.org/sls/31answers. htm. Accessed and vetted 26 November 2010, 08 December 2011.

Morse, Samuel F.B. 1855. *Foreign Conspiracy Against the Liberties of the United States. American and Foreign Christian Union.* New York, NY. [originally published in 1835, in the *New York Observer.*]

Mufti, S. and Shah, G.N. 2011. "Solar-geomagnetic activity influence on Earth's climate." *Journal of Atmospheric and Solar-Terrestrial Physics,* 73:13, pp. 1607-1615.

Mullins, Eustace. 1991. *Secrets of the Federal Reserve: The London Connection.* Bridger House Publishers, Inc. Carson City, NV.

Munn, O.D. 1884. [Notes by the Editor.] *Scientific American,* 13 September 1884, p. 161. New York, NY.

Murphy, Bill. 11 April 2010. Personal interview conducted by William Dean A. Garner.

Niles, H. 1834. "Deposites and Pensions." *Niles' Weekly Register,* March 1, 1834. Baltimore, MD.

Omerbashich, Mesur. 2007. "Magnification of mantle resonance as a cause of tectonics." *Geodinamica Acta.* 20:6, pp. 369-383.

Omerbashich, Mesur. 2011. "Astronomical alignments as the cause for ~M6+ seismicity." lanl.arxiv.org/pdf/1104.2036v5. Accessed and vetted 18 December 2011.

Owen, Robert Latham. 1919. *Where Is God in the European War?* The Century Company. New York, NY.

Paine, Thomas. 1776. *Common Sense: Which was Ordered by Congress to be Read at the Head of all Her Armies Before the Declaration of Independence, and by Washington at the Head of Every Captain's Company.* Philadelphia, PA.

Perkins, John. 2004. *Confessions of an Economic Hit Man.* Plume (Penguin). New York, NY.

"Planetary Influence Upon Solar Activity." *The American Annual Cyclopaedia and Register of Important Events of the Year 1872.* Volume 12, p. 38. D. Appleton and Company. New York, NY.

Powell, Chris and Murphy, William. 25 March 2010. "A London trader walks the CFTC through a silver manipulation in advance." www.gata.org/node/8466. Accessed and vetted 15 April 2010, 08 December 2011.

Prakash, Atul. 19 November 2007. "London ritual dating from 1919 sets price of gold." www.reuters.com/article/idUSL07289949200071119. Accessed and vetted 12 April 2010, 08 December 2011.

Proctor, Richard Anthony. 1883. *Rough Ways Made Smooth: A Series of Familiar Essays on Scientific Subjects.* Chatto and Windus. London, England.

Quigley, Carroll. 1966. *Tragedy and Hope: A History of the World in Our Time.* The Macmillan Company. New York, NY.

Ramsay, A.H.M. 1952. *The Nameless War.* The Britons Publishing Society. London, England.

Reed, George P. 1896. *The Crash of the Gold Combine, or Good Gold Cheap.* The Dawn Publishing Company. Chicago, IL.

Schuster, Arthur. 1872. "Sun-spots and the Vine Crop." *Nature* 5, 501. London, England.

Schuster, Arthur. 1906. "The Periodicity of Sun-Spots." *The Astrophysical Journal* 23:2, pp. 101-109. Chicago, IL.

Seagrave, Sterling and Peggy. 2003. *Gold Warriors: America's Secret Recovery of Yamashita's Gold*. Verso. London, England.

Seagrave, Sterling and Peggy. 13 April 2010. Personal interview conducted by William Dean A. Garner.

Self, Robert. 2006. *Neville Chamberlain: A Biography*. Ashgate Publishing, Ltd. Hants, England.

Skousen, W. Cleon. 1970. *The Naked Capitalist: A Review and Commentary on Dr. Carroll Quigley's Book: Tragedy and Hope-A History of the World in Our Time*. Privately published by W. Cleon Skousen. Salt Lake City, UT.

Sombart, Werner. 1913. *The Jews and Modern Capitalism*. E.P. Dutton and Company. New York, NY.

Stewart, Balfour. 1877. "Suspected Relations between the Sun and the Earth." *Nature*, Volume 16:393, pp. 26-28. London, England.

"Sun-spots and the Cholera." *The American Annual Cyclopaedia and Register of Important Events of the Year 1872*. Volume 12, p. 37. D. Appleton and Company. New York, NY.

"Sun-spots and the Vine Crop." *The American Annual Cyclopaedia and Register of Important Events of the Year 1872*. Volume 12, p. 37. D. Appleton and Company. New York, NY.

Sunstein, Cass R. and Vermeule, Adrian. 2008. "Conspiracy Theories." seanmaclarenbooks.com/wp-content/uploads/2015/06/SSRN-id1084585. pdf. Accessed and vetted 20 June 2015.

Sutter, John. 1857. In "The Discovery of Gold In California." *Hutchings' California Magazine*. Hutchings and Rosenfield. San Francisco, CA.

Sutton, Anthony. 2005. *The Federal Reserve Conspiracy*. Bridger House Publishers, Inc. Carson City, NV

"Testimony of Congressman Oscar Callaway." February 9, 1917. *The Congressional Record*. Vol. 54, pp. 2947-2948. Washington, DC.

United Nations Framework Convention on Climate Change. 1992. United Nations. New York, NY.

United States Congressional Record, 1-11 June 1932, U.S. Government Printing Office. Washington, DC

Williams, John. 19 November 2007. "Annual Inflation Surge Should Continue Inflation-Adjusted (SGS) Peak Gold Price Is $6,030." *Shadow Government Statistics*. www.shadowstats.com/article/aa935. Accessed and vetted 12 April 2010, 08 December 2011.

Williams, John. 02 December 2009. "Hyperinflation Special Report (Update 2010), Commentary Number 263: Economy and Financial System Face Eventual Great Collapse." *Shadow Government Statistics*. www.shadowstats.com/article/hyperinflation-2010. Accessed and vetted 12 April 2010, 08 December 2011.

Williams, John. 15 March 2011. "Hyperinflation Special Report (2011) Special Commentary Number 357: United States Nears Hyperinflationary Great Depression." *Shadow Government Statistics*. www.shadowstats.com/article/hyperinflation-special-report-2011.pdf. Accessed and vetted 08 December 2011

Wilson, Derek. 1988. *Rothschild: The Wealth and Power of a Dynasty*. Charles Scribner's Sons. New York, NY.

Wilson, Woodrow. 1913. *The New Freedom: A Call For the Emancipation of the Generous Energies of a People*. Doubleday, Page & Company. New York, NY

NOTE: A more extensive bibliography on the Jesuits can be found in Sean Maclaren's books, *Arcanum* and *Romanic Depression*, both available in paperback from Amazon.com and ebook from WilliamDeanAGarner.com, AdagioPress.com and SeanMaclarenBooks.com.

www.ingramcontent.com/pod-product-compliance
Lightning Source LLC
Chambersburg PA
CBHW020837210326
41598CB00019B/1936